Tales and Legends about Mathematical & Scientific Insights

Igor Ushakov

THE MAGIC OF GEOMETRY

San Diego
2012

Series

"Stories and Legends about Mathematical Insights"

Book 1. Man's first steps takes us through the first use of scientific and mathematical thinking as man began to question the nature of his Universe and then takes us into the history of measurements of the physical quantities of temperature, length, time and mass.

Book 2. In the beginning was the number … You find here new facts about Roman and Arabic numbers and some interesting methods of calculations. You also find here interesting things about magic numbers.

Book 3. The Magic of Geometry shows how the common problems of measuring land led to the development of mathematical discipline. You will know about unusual and impossible figures. You will have a pleasure to look at fantastic fractals.

Book 4. Enigmatic Terra Al-Jabr tells the stories of the origin and formation of algebra. You find from here that it is really interesting branch of mathematics.

Book 5. It's a Random, Random, Random World presents entertaining stories about the development of probability and statistics theory.

These books help teachers make their classes more interesting and help pupils to know even more than their teachers!

Cover design: Igor A. Ushakov.

To my beloved granddaughters
Anastasia & Alisa

Preface

The subject of mathematics is so serious that nobody should miss an opportunity to make it a little bit entertaining.

Blaise Pascal [1].

What is this book about? For whom is it written? Why is it written in this manner, not in another? Discussion about geometry, algebra and similar topics definitely hint that this is about mathematics. On the other hand, you cannot find within a proof of any statement or strong chronology of facts. Thus, this is not a tutorial book on mathematics or on of mathematics. This is just a collection of interesting and sometimes exciting stories and legends about human discoveries in one or another way connected to mathematics…

Our book is open for everybody who likes to enrich their intelligence with the stories of genius insights and great mistakes (mistakes also can be great!), and with biographies of creators of mathematical thinking and mathematical approaches in the study of the World.

Who are the readers of the proposed book? We believe that there is no special audience in the sense of education or age. The books could be interesting to schoolteachers and university professors (not necessarily mathematicians!) who would like to make their lectures more vivid and intriguing. At the same time, students of different educational levels as well as their parents may find here many interesting facts and ideas. We can imagine that the book could be interesting even for state leaders whose educational level is enough to read something beyond speeches prepared for them by their advisors.

Trust us: we tried to write the book clearly! Actually, it is non-mathematical book around mathematics.

---

[1] **Blaise Pascal** (1623 –1662) was a French mathematician, physicist, inventor, writer and philosopher.

This book is not intended to convert you to a "mathematical religion". Indeed, there is no need to do this: imagine how boring life would be if everybody were a mathematician? Mathematics is the world of ideas, however any idea needs to be realized: integrals cannot appease your hunger, differential equations cannot fill gas tank of your car....

However, to be honest, we pursued the objective: we tried to convince you, the reader, that without mathematics *homo erectus* would never transform into *homo sapiens.*

Now, let us travel into the very interesting place: Terra Mathematica. We'll try to make this your trip interesting and exciting.

Igor Ushakov

Contents

Contents

1 NEW GEOMETRY 7

1.1 TWO-DIMENSIONAL LINE?!.. 7
1.2 SNOWFLAKES, NAPKINS, PYRAMIDS… 12
1.3 FRACTAL GEOMETRY....19
1.4 CHAOS....25
1.5 SELF-SIMILARITY....30
1.6 FRACTALS, FRACTALS, EVERYWHERE ONLY FRACTALS… 31

2 UNUSUAL AND IMPOSSIBLE FIGURES 36

2.1 MOEBIUS STRIP....36
2.2 LET US PLAY WITH MEOBIUS STRIP! 38
2.3 MOEBIUS "FRAMES"....42
2.4 KLEIN BOTTLE 46
2.5. INFINITELY ENCLOSED KLEIN "MUG" 47
2.5 IMPOSSIBLE FIGURES....51
2.6 MATHEMATICS AND FINE ART 56

3 "GOLDEN SECTION"....62

3.1 HISTORY OF THE "GOLDEN SECTION" 63
3.2 HOW TO CONSTRUCT THE GOLDEN SECTION....68
3.3 "GOLDEN SECTION" IN NATURE....74
3.4 "GOLDEN SECTION" IN ART 78
3.5 FIBONACCI NUMBERS 81

4 PYTHAGOREAN GEOMETRY 87

4.1 PYTHAGORAS' THEOREM 87
4.2 THE PROOF OF THE PYTHAGORAS' THEOREM....90

PANTHEON 92

PYTHAGORAS OF SAMOS 92
LEONARDO FIBONACCI....101
FRA LUCA BARTOLOMEO DE PACIOLI....105
LEONARDO DA VINCI....109

NEW GEOMETRY

Why is geometry often described as "cold" and "dry"?

One reason lies in its inability to describe the shape of a cloud, a mountain, a coastline, a tree... Clouds are not spheres, mountains are not cones, coastlines are not circles, and bark is not smooth, nor does lightning travel in a straight line.

B. Mandelbrot [2].

1.1 Two-dimensional line?!..

So, the naturalists observe, the flea,
Hath smaller fleas that on him prey;
And these have smaller still to bite 'em;
And so proceed, ad infinitum[3].

Jonathan Swift [4]

From school, we know that a line has one dimension, that a plane has two dimensions, and that we live in a world of three spatial dimensions. This is obvious …

However, in mathematics the word "obvious" is not acceptable: what looks[5] like the truth is not necessarily true.

In 1890 Peano[6] developed a principle for constructing a two-dimensional continuous curve. This curve fills a restricted square and runs through all the points on the square. Doubtlessly, such a curve would

---

[2] **Benoit Mandelbrot** (1924-2011) was an American mathematician, creator of a new direction in computer graphics – fractal geometry.
[3] *Ad infinitum* in Latin means "*until infinity*".
[4] **Jonathan Swift** (1667-1745) was an Anglo-Irish writer who is famous for "Gulliver's Travels". He is probably the foremost prose satirist in the English language.
[5] "Evident" is from French word "*videns*" that comes from the Latin "*videre*", which means "*to see*".
[6] **Giuseppe Peano** (1858-1932) was an Italian mathematician, one of the founders of Symbolic logic. He developed a set of axioms on natural numbers.

require infinite time to construct, but, what mathematician cares about such practical considerations? For them, it is sufficient to note that, in principle, it is possible to do so!

Peano's method consists of the following: a given square is divided into nine equal squares. One constructs a curve that looks like the letter "*N*", which runs through each of the nine small squares. The procedure continues as is depicted below.

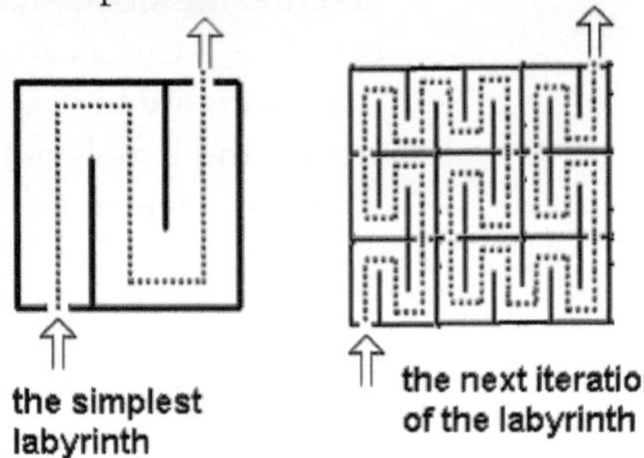

A recurrent procedure is applied; the curve exiting from the previous square enters the neighboring square.

Greek mythology tells us how Theseus killed the Minotaur in a Labyrinth designed by Daedal. He used Ariadna's ball of yarn to lay a trail that he could then retrace to find his way back to the exit from the Labyrinth. Had this Labyrinth been designed by Peano, Ariadna would never have found enough yarn in all of Greece (or the universe) to help Theseus.

There is another method to construct a Peano Labyrinth. The same "generator" in the form of an N-type curve is used, but with a different rule for the "exit-entrance" connection. This new rule for Peano's Labyrinth construction is shown below: the difference is evident just from the visual comparison of two pictures

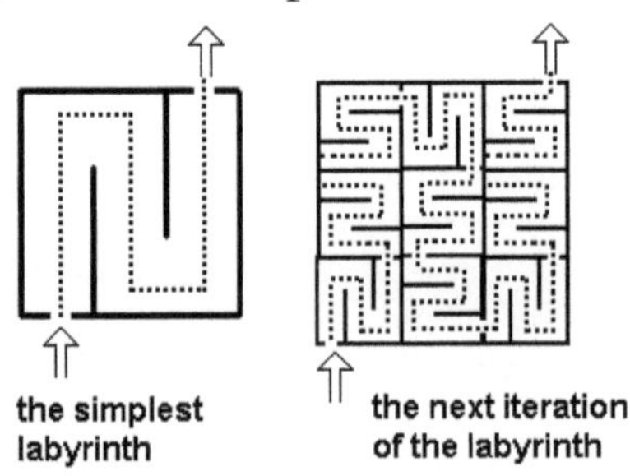

Both Peano's Labyrinths curves have the "entrances" and "exits" on the opposite sides of the square, so these curves sometimes are called "*diagonal*."

In 1891 Hilbert constructed his well-known curve – the so-called "Hilbert's Hotel," which resembles Peano's Labyrinth. Sometimes this curve, justifiably, is called the "Peano-Hilbert" curve, but we'll keep the original name.

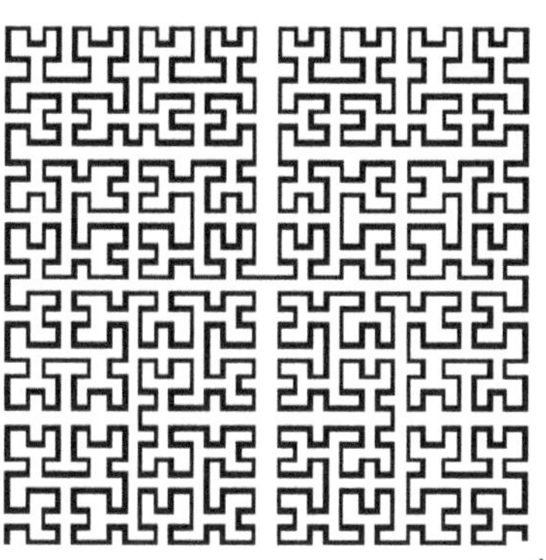

How might one construct a "Hilbert's Hotel?" First, divide a square into four equal squares. Within these four squares, construct the simplest labyrinth and draw a path through all four squares.

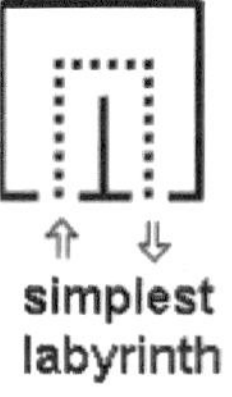

simplest labyrinth

After which, each small square from the original is divided into four new smaller squares and in the labyrinth a new path is constructed.

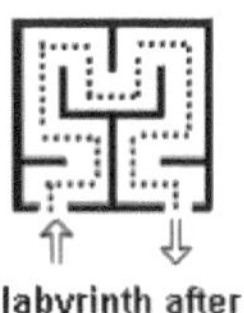

labyrinth after the first iteration

Proceed again to divide the squares and it would look like the following picture (on the left).

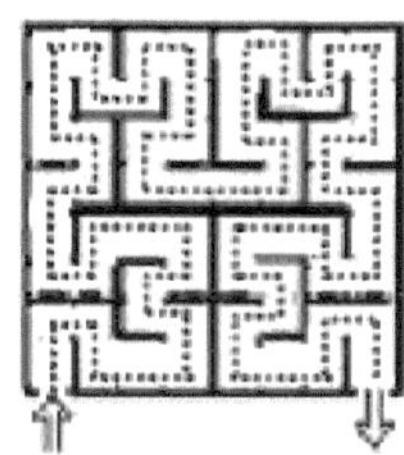

labyrinth after the second iteration

This process continues infinitely as the path runs through smaller and smaller squares, contained entirely within the initial square. Notice that at each step of the iterative process, the "entrance" and the "exit" are located on the same side of the initial square.

Continuing the procedure infinitely, we will get Hilbert's Hotel, which as well as Peano's Curve, will run through all points of the plane defined by the initial square.

David Hilbert

(1852-1943)

German mathematician, who is often called the last person to know all of mathematics. He made great contributions in various branches of mathematics. It is believed that his contributions to geometry are probably second only to that of the great ancient mathematician, Euclid.

Hilbert famously published and presented a table of 23 problems (the so-called "Hilbert's Problems"), of which several are still a solution in 21st century for. Twenty-one of them have been solved.

Now we remind you that this one dimensional curve contains all the points in our two-dimensional square!

In a sense, an "inverse" construction has been suggested by Cantor. He constructed an infinite set of "isolated" points. This set is called "Cantor's Dust".

Georg Ferdinand Ludwig Philipp Cantor

(1845-1918)

German mathematician and founder of Set Theory. Developed the theory of infinite sets; proved that all real numbers form an uncountable set; formulated a concept of the power of a set. He proved the existence of transcendental numbers. The Set Theory created by Cantor led to the revision of the logical basis of mathematics.

David Hilbert said about him: "Nobody can expel us from the Eden, which Cantor created for us".

The procedure to construct Cantor's set, which is denoted by *K*, is as follows: Take a segment, for instance, of length 1. Divide it into three equal parts and exclude the middle part. Perform the same procedure with the remaining two segments (see the figure below).

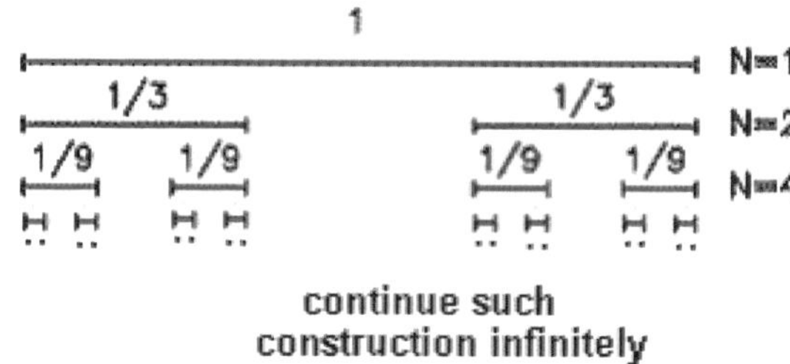

Let us continue the procedure infinitely, giving us the Cantor Set *K*. Between any two points of this set there are points which do not belong to the set. Continuing the procedure infinitely leads to the formation of the so-called "Cantor's Dust", the length of which is equal to 0.

"Cantor's comb" can be constructed in the same manner,. The beginning of the construction of "Cantor's Comb" is shown below.

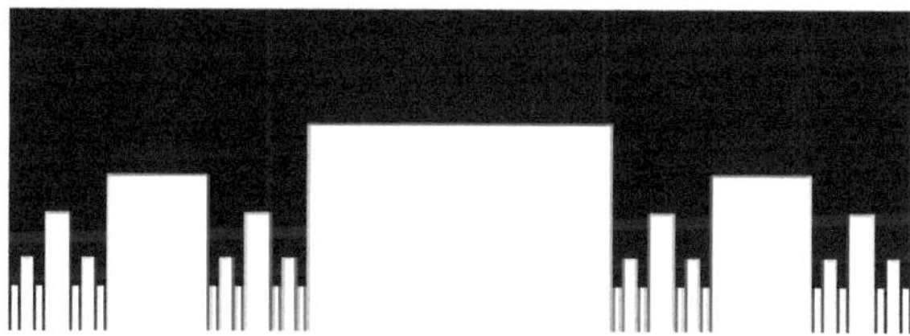

With the growing number of "teeth," the comb transforms into an infinitely long "broom."

Let's get back to the topic of construction of infinitely long curves restricted by some closed area on the plane.

1.2 Snowflakes, napkins, pyramids…

In the very beginning of the 20th century another mathematician, Niels Koch,[7] studying works by Cantor and Weierstrass[8], constructed a curve with strange properties. He found this by doing the following: He took a segment, divided it into three equal parts and built an equilateral triangle on the middle part. Then he continued the procedure with four segments obtained after the first step, and so on.

Notice that Koch's curve is continuous, but yet it does not have a tangent at any point.

Koch also built the so-called "Koch's Snowflake," or "Koch's Star." This figure can be constructed in the following way: Take an equilateral triangle and divide each side into three equal segments. At this first step we obtain a figure, which is recognized as the "Star of David9." The process continues as shown in the figure below.

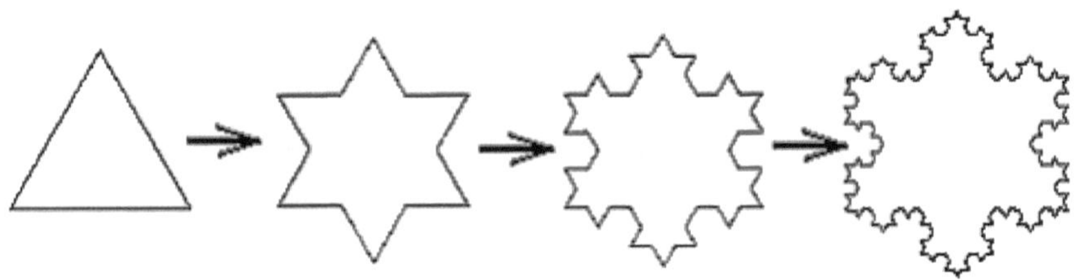

[7] **Niels Fabian Helge von Koch** (1870-1924) was a Swedish mathematician, specialist in the Theory of Numbers.

[8] **Karl Theodor Wilhelm Weierstrass** (1815-1897)was a German mathematician whose works had played significant role for mathematics developing.

[9] Star of David, or more accurately, the Shield of David ("Magen David") is a hexagram. Magen David serves as an emblem of Judaism. However, the origin of this symbol is unknown: the Shield of David is never mentioned either in the Bible or in the Talmud. Moreover, Judaism forbids the use of images or symbols.

Koch's snowflake is a continuous curve, which does not have a tangent at any point. It is infinite and surrounds a limited area. Naturally, almost immediately this led to the appearance of new fancy figures. Probably, the first one was the "Minkovski Cross".

Hermann Minkovski

(1864-1909)

Lithuanian mathematician who first considered four dimensions, "the space-time continuum." In one of his later works he formulated "Principle of relativity."

When Minkovski had been lecturing in Zurich, one of the attendants was Albert Einstein who was impressed by those lectures. The lectures influenced Einstein when he created his Theory of Relativity.

Below is another infinite continuous curve construction that has no tangents at any point on the curve. The first few steps in the construction of this curve are shown below.

This figure is known as «*Minkovski's Sausage*», a term that doubtlessly was invented afterwards by some mathematical wit. As one can see from the picture, that while Koch chose an equilateral triangle as the "generating element," Minkovski chose a square.

The "Durer's Star" was named after the famous Renaissance German artist who developed a construction method for a pentagon, which is the generation seed for this curve. We avoid a detail description of this construction limiting ourselves to presenting the drawings below.

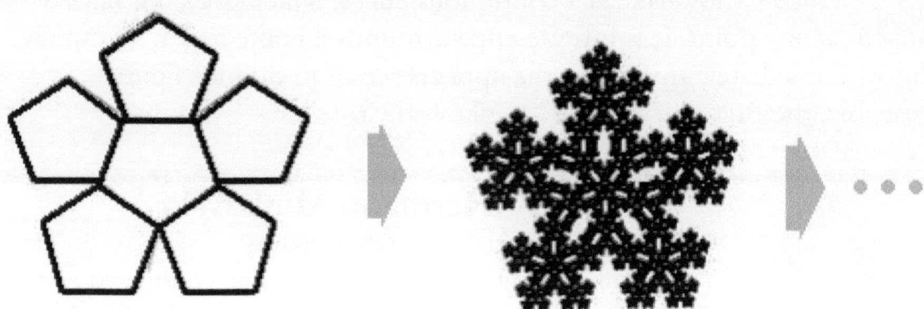

Following this, exotic geometrical figures were constructed not by a growth of lines but by the extraction of some restricted areas from the initial figure. In 1915 Sierpinski[10] suggested the construction of an object, which now bears his name – "Sierpinski's Triangle."

Three first steps of the constructing are given below.

The number of triangle holes that can be made by this method, of course, is infinite. The number of black triangles increases as 3n where n is the number of iterations; the length of their sides decreases as 2^{-n}. The limit of the total area occupied by white triangles becomes equal to the area of the initial triangle.

Another analogous geometrical object, "Sierpinski's Carpet" is constructed by taking a square and dividing it into nine

[10] **Wraclav Sierpinski** (1882–1969) was a Polish mathematician.

equally sized squares. Expel the central square. Repeat the procedure with each of the remaining eight squares. In the final result, we get a grid consisting of an infinitesimally thin rectangular "web" with no remaining area. Usually, this object is called "Sierpinski's Sieve".

As an aside, Martin Gardner[11] mentioned that in 1905 at an annual mathematical Olympiad for schoolchildren in Hungary there was a test: "A square is divided into 9 equal squares (like for tick-tack-toe) and then the central square is deleted. Then the procedure is repeated infinitely. Find the value of the remaining area in the limit as the iterations go to infinity." Poor school children! It likely was not an appropriate "joke" on the part of the teacher; students did not know anything about infinitesimals.

Such intriguing construction techniques are also valid in 3-dimensional space. For instance, the 3-dimensional version of "Serpinski's Triangle" – "Serpinski's Pyramid" can be obtained if one takes a tetrahedron and cuts out from it smaller and smaller tetrahedrons, as shown below.

In this process the pyramid consists of "holes" yet its "skeleton" continues to exist!

"Serpinski's Sieve" in 3 dimensional space becomes "Sierpinski's Sponge," which is constructed in a manner similar to the construction of "Serpinski's Pyramid" above. From the initial cube, one removes a 3-dimensional cross section consisting of the following form:

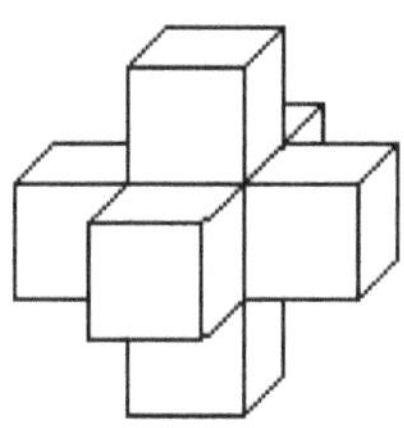

[11] **Martin Gardner** (1914-2010) was an American mathematician and science writer.

A figure consisting of 20 smaller cubes is left. In the figure below you see "Sierpinski's Sponge" after three iterations.

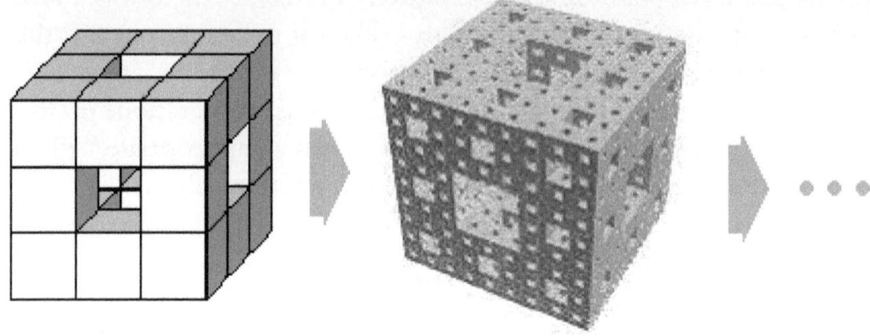

In this case the same fancy effect happens: The initial cube after an infinite number of steps will consist of square holes with a frame of seemingly infinitesimally thin strings.

1.3 Fractal geometry

> There is no such a big thing that there is no a bigger one. At the same time there is no such a small thing that there is no a smaller one.
>
> ***Unknown author***

The area of enigmatic constructions was literally invaded by mathematics. In the beginning of the twentieth century two mathematicians – Pierre Fatou[12] and Gaston Julia[13] – simultaneously and

[12] **Pierre Josef Fatou** (1878 - 1929) was a French mathematician, specialist in functions of complex arguments. He formulated in 1905 a described above procedure that has been used later by B. Mandelbrot for construction fractals.

[13] **Gaston Julia** (1893-1978) was a French mathematician discovered a property of self-

independently investigated asymptotic (limit) behavior of sets generated on the complex plane by some special recurrent procedures.

Let us remind that a complex number $z = a+bi$ consists of real and imaginary parts. The imaginary part includes the so called "imaginary unit": $i = \sqrt{-1}$. Real numbers, "a" and "b", are reflected on the numerical axes, while complex numbers are plotted on the complex plane. On the complex plane, a real part is located on the abscissa (horizontal axis) and an imaginary part plotted on the ordinate (vertical axis), so any complex number is reflected by a point on the complex plane.

Now let us return to a recurrent procedure mentioned above. This procedure in general form can be written as follows:

$$z_{n+1} = f(z_n).$$

Let $z_{n+1} = z_n^2 + c$,

where c is a complex parameter. Let us remind how to get power 2 of a complex number $z = a+bi$:

$$z^2=(a+bi)\cdot(a+bi)=a^2+abi+abi+(bi)^2=a^2+2abi-b^2=(a^2-b^2)+2abi.$$

Let us start with the simplest value of constant c, namely, with $c = 0$. Then for each iteration we calculate an exact square of the number:

$$z_0 \Rightarrow z_0^2 \Rightarrow z_0^4 \Rightarrow \dots .$$

For this sequence, depending on the originally chosen point z_0 on the complex plane there are three possibilities:

1. If the distance from z_0 to the origin is smaller than 1, then the sequence of powers of z_0 goes to its *attractor*, i.e. to the so-called "point of gravity" – zero.

2. If z_0 locates outside the circle with the radius equal to 1, that located around the origin, then the sequence of powers of z_0 begins to run out to the infinity. In this case, the attractor is the infinity.

---

similarity for boundaries of the Fatou's sets and constructed such boundaries.

3. If z_0 locates on the circle with radius equal to 1, then all powers of z_0 will locate on the circle, i.e. the circle itself will be an attractor.

However, if one chooses non-zero parameter c, for instance,

$$c = -0{,}12 + 0{,}56i,$$

then the there will be same three possibilities, though the inner sequence's attractor will be not zero and the boundary will not be smooth. One of the properties of such boundaries is self-similarity. If one looks at a fragment of such a trajectory, it is possible to notice that similar or almost similar shape of the curve appears in different places though could have different size. The most interesting case is the boundary between order and chaos. Those boundaries are called Fatou-Julia's sets.

Julia described wrote about properties of these boundaries and tried to construct simplest of them; however he never even guessed how daedal they are! Only recently with the advent of computers have researchers begun to look at these boundaries. Some examples of the mentioned boundaries are provided below.

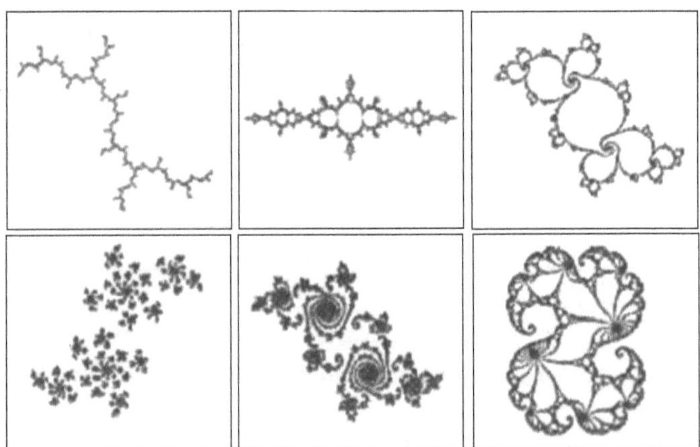

Thus, we came to the concept of *fractals*. What does fractal mean? For better understanding, let us first remember their "ancestry". You may consider that the Peano Curve and Hilbert Hotel were "parents" of the Fatou-Julia Sets are the "parents" of Mandelbrot's fractals. However, it takes about fifty years for fractals to appear: their construction is so complicated and nearly impossible without computers.

Benoit Mandelbrot

(1924-2011)

American mathematician, creator of a new direction in computer graphics – fractal geometry. He was born in Warsaw (Poland) and educated in France where his uncle was one of the mathematicians who formed the famous group that had a collective pseudonym, Nicolas Bourbaki. Mandelbrot was a Professor at Yale and employee of the IBM Research Center. He simultaneously was a member of National Academy and American Academy of Fine Art.

So, what is it: fractal? For non-mathematicians fractals are enigmatic geometrical figures that almost 50 years are subjects of astonishing and admiration people of all ages. The term "*fractal*" was invented and coined by Benoit Mandelbrot – "the father of fractal geometry". The word is originated from Latin «*fractus*» that means fragmentary or consisting of fragments.

Mandelbrot knew works by Fatou and Julia very well and successfully developed their methods. Moreover, Mandelbrot paid tributes to Gustav Julia whose name was mostly forgotten by the mathematical community.

Using computer modeling, Mabdelbrot began to construct his wonderful fractals. The figure below was his first "child" and is commonly known as "Mandelbrot's fractal".

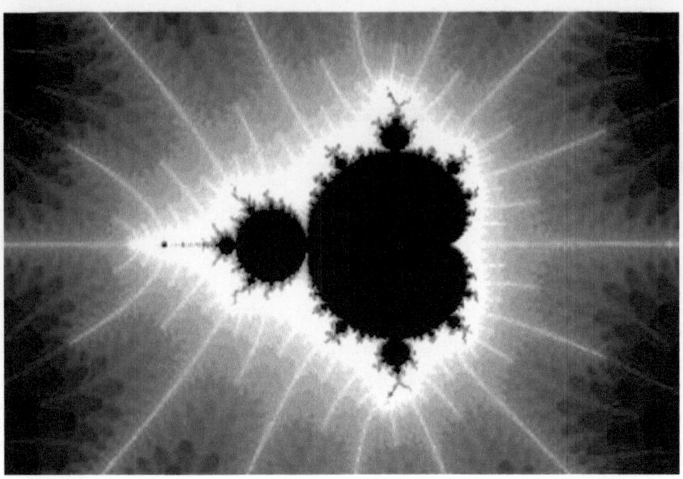

However, Mandelbrot's active interest in fractals was inspired by the work of Luis Richardson[14] who mentioned that the length of the coastline of the West part of Great Britain strongly depends on the scale. The larger scale, the more details can be seen: small curves, small capes and bays. At the same time, maps with small scales have no such details, they are lost due to the "smoothing" effect. In other words, the coastline length depends on what map you take to measure it!

We decided "to kill two birds with a single stone": to show you how a coastline changes with the change of scale and simultaneously to demonstrate how fractal changes its ornament with increasing its size. We hope that pictures below needs no comments: both sets of pictures have, in some sense, "similar" characters of changes with scale decrease.

[14] **Lewis Fry Richardson** (1881-1953) was an English mathematician and meteorologist published his works in 1920-s.

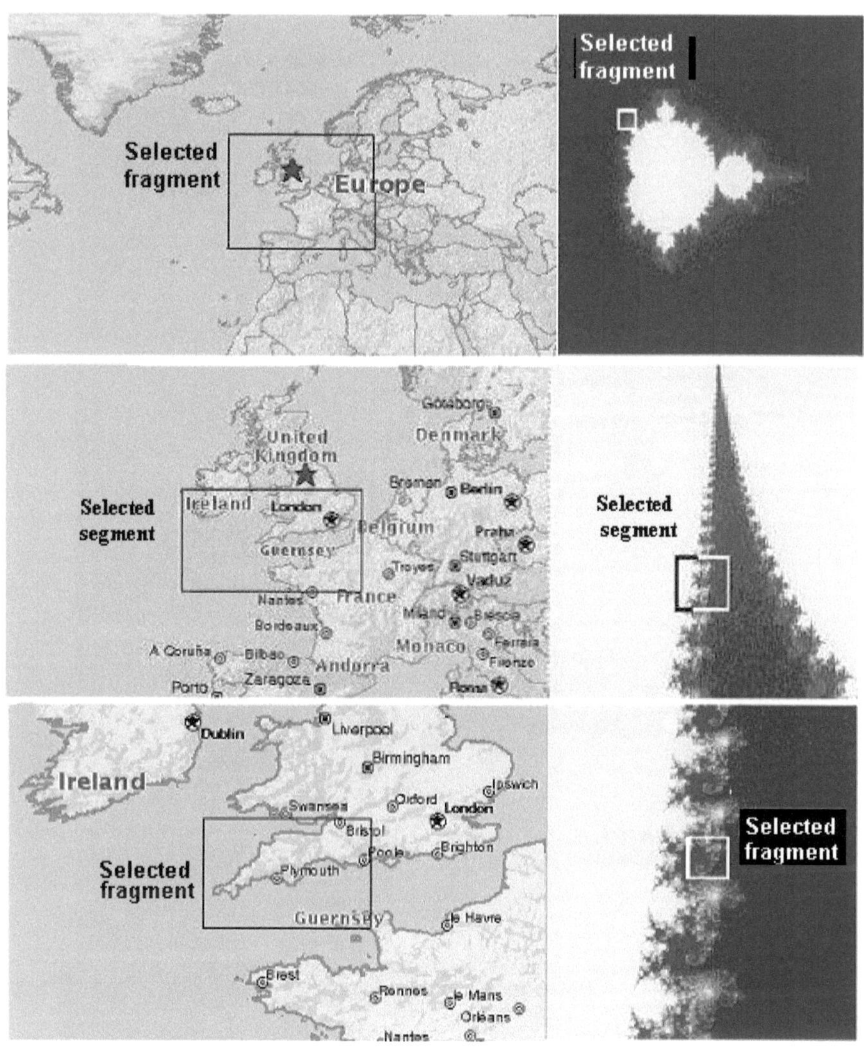
Selected
fragment
Europe
Selected
fragment
United
Kingdom
Denmark
Ireland
London
Belgium
Guernsey
France
Andorra
Monaco
Selected
segment
Selected
segment
Dublin
Liverpool
Ireland
Birmingham
Swansea
Oxford
London
Ipswich
Bristol
Brighton
Plymouth
Guernsey
Le Havre
Brest
Rennes
Le Mans
Orléans
Nantes
Selected
fragment
Selected
fragment

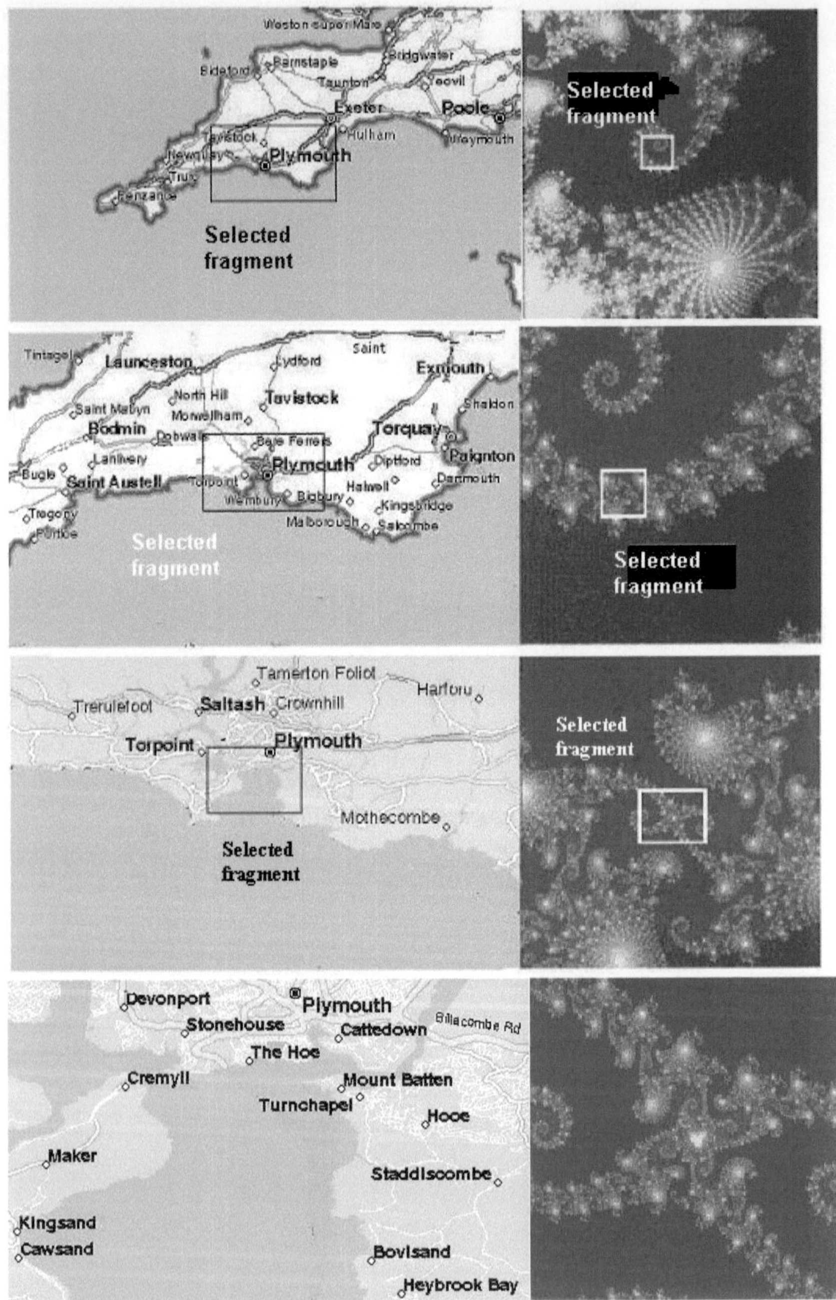
Selected fragment
Bideford
Barnstaple
Bridgwater
Taunton
Yeovil
Exeter
Poole
Plymouth
Weymouth
Selected fragment
Launceston
Tavistock
Exmouth
Torquay
Bodmin
Saint Austell
Plymouth
Paignton
Selected fragment
Selected fragment
Tamerton Foliot
Saltash
Crownhill
Torpoint
Plymouth
Mothecombe
Selected fragment
Selected fragment
Devonport
Plymouth
Stonehouse
Cattedown
The Hoe
Cremyll
Mount Batten
Turnchapel
Hooe
Maker
Staddiscombe
Kingsand
Cawsand
Bovisand
Heybrook Bay

The concept of fractals was introduced by Mandelbrot in 1977 in his book "The Fractal Geometry of the Nature" where he generalized the works of his predecessors and introduced a significant leap forward.

One can find software for fractals drawing in the Internet (just type the word "fractal" and you'll get tens of related programs!).

1.4 Chaos

... And the earth was without form, and void;
and darkness was upon the face of deep...
The Bible, *"Genesis"*.

What could chaos and the most precise discipline, mathematics, have in common? Mathematicians have found a way to describe the "mathematical structure" of chaos and have developed a rigorous definition of chaos.

We begin with a known phenomenon: Everybody knows the so-called "microphone effect;" as a microphone is brought closer to a speaker's mouth, one hears the nasty gnashing and whistling of feedback. This phenomenon occurs because an avalanche process begins. What starts out as negligible noise from the speaker is picked up by the microphone, then amplified and sent out to the speaker, which sends the amplified sound back to the microphone and loops creating an avalanche that is bound only by the limitations of equipment. This process is called a positive feedback.

Mandelbrot was the first to pay attention to the phenomenon of chaos. While he was working at a computer company, he dealt with influence of telephone line noise on computer modems. He began to build a mathematical model describing noise phenomenon. Modem errors were chaotic and unpredictable and could not be described by any known mathematical model. This discouraging fact would depress almost anybody but not Mandelbrot, who spotted some hint of self-similarity. Let's digress for a moment and look at some common and important examples of self-similarity. Local weather has great similarities to regional weather which in turn has great similarities to weather in adjacent regions. In history "the great Renaissance" consists of smaller events of discovery or progress, each of which collectively sum to the global process. In other words, chaotic systems appear to contain within themselves self-similar smaller parts; these smaller parts, in turn, consist of even smaller parts similar to the larger parts.

Although we typically understand "chaos" to mean disorder and unpredictability, it is reasonable to ask, "How much of chaos is chaotic?" In spite of the seemingly contradictory sense of this question, we can say that chaos is sufficiently ordered and follows definite laws. The problem is that defining these laws is typically very difficult.

In the last few decades the Theory of Chaos successfully has been developed with application to dynamic systems. A dynamic system is such a system which changes state in time, typically in a manner described by mathematical rules expressed by equations that predict the future system state (or behavior) based on observations or measurement of its previous state and behavior. Such a system is deterministic if the rules do not include factors of randomness. Though if these deterministic rules of behavior are extremely complex, the system's behavior seems random and even unpredictable.

Up until about 1960 most of physicists and other specialists believed that a mechanical dynamic system described by simple deterministic rules should exhibit relatively simple behavior. However, mathematicians and naturalists found that chaos is inherent in all systems.

One of the key essential properties of dynamic systems is repetition of the system behavior in accordance with some known algorithm. System states are characterized by a number or a set of numbers; for instance, a system coordinate might change in accordance with the rule, "raise an initial value to the second power." If one uses this rule starting with, say, the number 1/2, then the sequence generated will be 1/2 →1/4→ 1/16 → 1/256 →..., which follows a definite rule and which term converges (to zero in this case). The same rule applied to a number larger than one leads to a sequence that does not converge and each subsequent term grows to infinity; for instance: 1.5→ 2.25→ 5.0625→ 25.6289→ 656.8408→… If that same power rule is modified slightly, "raise an initial value to the second power and subtract one" and is applied to an initial value of 0, then the sequence –1, 0, –1, 0,..., is generated. This sequence exhibits regular "jumps" from 0 to –1 and back

A	B
-0.68	-0.9488
-0.0752	0.620797
-0.98869	-0.70295
0.955016	-0.51165
0.824109	-0.86293
0.358312	0.109017
-0.74322	-0.99972
0.104766	0.997741
-0.97805	0.981989
0.913156	0.859759
0.667709	0.092793
-0.10833	-0.99985
-0.97653	0.998814
0.907219	0.990529
0.646092	0.925302
-0.16513	0.466101
-0.94546	-0.9056
0.787807	0.345194
0.241279	-0.9716
-0.88357	0.782315
0.561389	-0.25087
-0.36968	-0.99208
-0.72667	0.937373
0.056089	0.544116

from –1 to 0. However, if one again slightly changes the rule, say, to, "raise an initial value to the second power, multiply the result by 2, and then subtract one", and one chooses 0.4 as the initial number, then the generated sequence of numbers will be as given in the column A of the table below. If one raises the same initial number into the fourth power, then the result will be like it is presented in column B of the same table.

The point of this last example, of course, is to illustrate that from the data it is nearly impossible to discern that there is a generating function. The obtained sequence seems rather random; well, at least, this is a good example of pseudo randomness in the segment [–1, 1].

One of the basic concepts in Chaos Theory is the attractor, i.e. some area in the set of system's states to which the system goes. We already saw that it might be zero or infinity; in another case it was the two numbers: –1 and 0. And in the last case the number characterizing the system belongs to the entire segment [–1, 1]. In this last case the attractor is said to be chaotic. The hidden structure of such a chaotic attractor can be seen only after graphical presentation. For this last case the graphic representation is shown below.

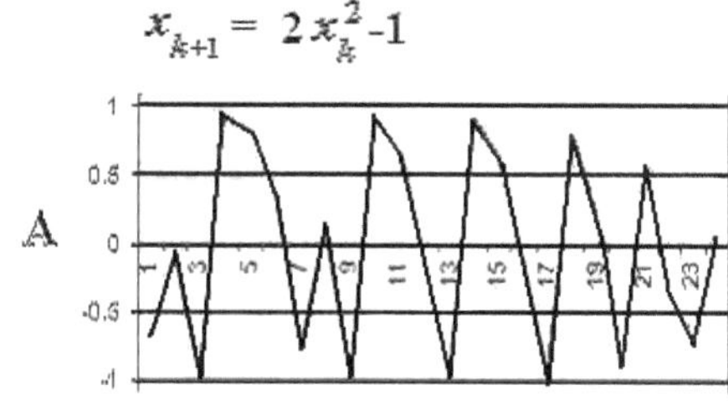

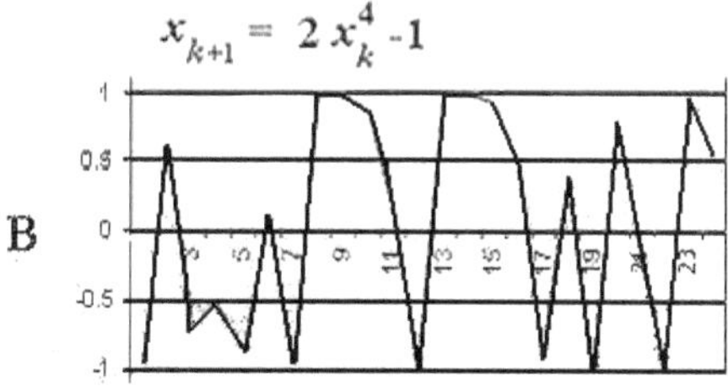

If one chooses a complex number as an initial point, then in the case of a chaotic attractor, the moving point will form a fancy configuration, which is called a *fractal.*

The mathematical concept of chaos had not been formulated until the 1960s; however, original sources are found in Poincare's works on the heavenly bodies moving in the Solar system.

Jules Henri Poincare

(1854-1912)

French mathematician, physicist, astronomer and philosopher. He and David Hilbert are considered as the "last Mathematical Universalists". In astronomy, Poincare's works deal with celestial mechanics and cosmology.

Simultaneously and independently he and Albert Einstein developed "relativity postulate".

Poincare was a member of Paris Academy of Sciences and an honorable member of the St. Petersburg Academy of Sciences.

Chaos Theory is widely applied in various sciences. Probably, one of the earliest applications relates to turbulence analysis in fluid flow[15].

Developments in meteorology demonstrate that atmospheric behavior is chaotic. This means that long-range prediction of the weather on the basis of previous observations is impossible because of the phenomenon of "butterfly effect".

Remark: The term "butterfly effect" was coined by American mathematician and meteorologist Edward Norton Lorenz (born 1917). In 1972 gave a talk "Predictability: Does the Flap of a Butterfly's Wings in Brazil set off a Tornado in Texas?"

The butterfly effect reflects the idea that small variations of the initial conditions of a dynamic system may lead to large-scale phenomena in the long term behavior of the system.

[15] Movement of liquid can be either laminar (smooth and regular) like in a big and deep river, or turbulent (impetuous and irregular) like in a rapidly running mountain creek.

Thus, modestly precise weather prediction is limited to a few days regardless of the volume of collected information and the power of computers engaged in the forecasting efforts.

Poincare noticed that the motion of celestial bodies was chaotic, though the process of changing their position is so slow that only events that happen in tens of million years are unpredictable. One of the brightest examples of such phenomenon with celestial bodies is Saturn's Moon, Hyperion: Its motion around the planet is regular; yet, it is chaotically somersaulting and chaotically changing the axis of its rotation.

Chaos is found in ecology and biology. Animal populations are rarely stable; they are subject to epochs of fast growth or near complete extinction. Chaos Theory shows that such fluctuation can be explained even without intervention of external factors. Chaos Theory also explains the dynamics of pandemics, i.e. the spontaneous random changing of microorganisms populations.

So, what is the point in having a theory about a process if it cannot predict the course of the process, as in chaotic systems? First, this theory provides new views of data that in some cases previously had been considered to be chaotic, i.e. having no rules of behavior. Furthermore, Chaos Theory supports the identification of "predictable components" in chaotic systems.

Methods of Chaos Theory initially were used successfully in "well-formalized" sciences like physics and chemistry; later these methods found wide application in traditionally humanitarian areas like psychology, sociology, and economics, where one needs to analyze the behavior of a huge number of objects (people, results of their activity, etc.) that interact chaotically to form a complete system.

1.5 Self-Similarity

Who is: A son of my father
though not my brother?

Joking question.

A self-similar figure is a figure that can be divided into a finite number of figures, each similar to the original one. Examples of such figures: equilateral triangle and square.

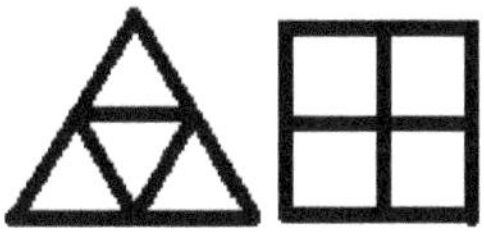

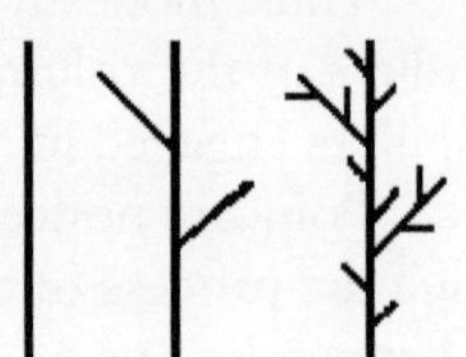

Many fancy figures exist with self-similarity properties, such as "a branch" presented in the figure on the right.

Analogous properties are found in Nature: coral reefs, mountains, clouds, cracks in sun baked mud, etc. In many cases one can find similarity of their parts with the entire object with the help of a magnifying glass. Benoit Mandelbrot named such objects "fractals".[16].

Thus, those objects considered in the previous section – from Peano's curve to Sierpinsky's sponge – all of them are fractals! Though, as one might say, they are primitive fractals, a «*fractus erectus*», so to speak. In that case, we could say that the complex fractals (those generated with computers) are «*fractus sapiens*».

1.6 Fractals, fractals, everywhere only fractals...

My name is legion : for we are many.
Saint Mark, Chapter 5

Above we mentioned the so-called *deterministic* fractals: These are built by a regular mathematical rule. However, *random fractals* also exist! A simple example is the track of a particle performing Brownian motion.

[16] From Latin word "fractus", meaning broken, divided into pieces.

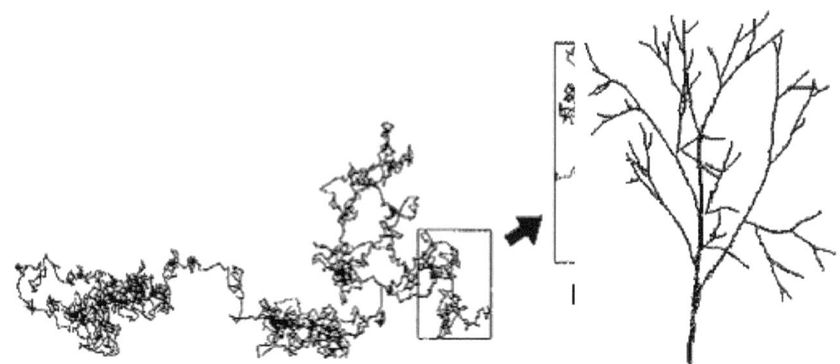

A Brownian track has a very complex and unpredictable nature, though, if one increases the scale, it can be seen that the fragment of the track has astonishing similarity to the whole track!

An example of a fractal that is "random but not totally so" is tree branches which are grow with increasing "noise" in the construction process.

This figure possesses the properties:

1. Each segment is similar to the whole.
2. Each fragment allows infinite expansion while preserving the "typical properties" of the whole object.

Because they describe the real world sometimes even better than traditional physics and mathematics, fractals have taken over many aspects of science. Here are some examples: In computer science one of the most effective applications of fractals is in compressing data. The underlying reason that fractals work well for compression is that the real world is well described by fractal geometry. Photographs compress better with algorithms based on fractals than they do with typical methods such as JPEG. Another advantage of fractal compression is that the process of "decompression" does not cause picture distortion because the generator is fundamental and specific to the photograph, unlike the standard fits all Discrete Cosine Transform ("generator") of JPEG compression. Literally, the picture after enlarging looks better than before!

Turbulent flows found in fluid systems and flames are some examples of common place chaotic physical processes that are modeled usefully by fractals.

The applicability of fractals to medicine is a natural consequence of the fact that the human lung, brain, circulatory system, etcetera have a fractal structure. Wide applications of fractals to cardiology already have been found.

Fractals have penetrated into other spheres of human activity. For instance, an exhibition of pictures, titled "Coming to Chaos," by Eric Heller, chemistry and physics professor at Harvard University, had a long tour through the United States. The author used in his art approaches of modern fractal geometry. Some of his pictures – they are, indeed, interesting – are shown below.

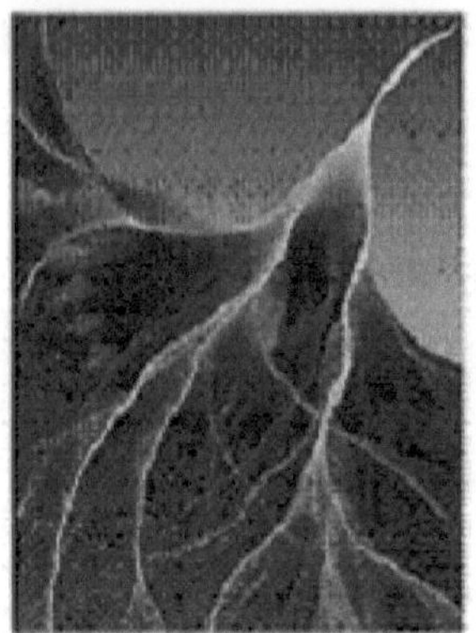

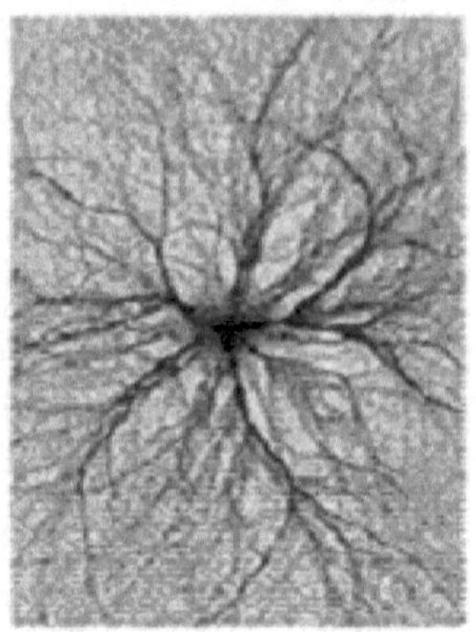

Such "pure mathematical" art is beautiful in a sense but is not unexpected after

Mandelbrot's works. Fractal methodology is widely used in various fantastic movies in which various unusual mountain landscapes, waterfalls and exotic plants are created with the help of computer programs based on fractal geometry. And these attempts are really intriguing because man has been eager to create "artificial intelligence."

An example of a 3-dimensional landscape synthesized by Martin Murphy using a software program, *Bryce*, based on fractals, is shown below.

Clouds, mountains, trees, light and shadows are realistic, aren't they? Note that Mandelbrot, the father of fractal geometry, contributed significantly to the creation of this program.

Many artists intuitively sensed the fractal dimension/nature of real objects. Leonardo da Vinci even formulated an interesting rule that is understandable in a fractal framework: All the branches of a tree at some fixed distance from the tree trunk gathered together in total have the same mass of wood as the trunk below. This observation is in accordance with the definition of branching.

Naturally, the analogous arguments can be applied to music as well as the sounds of the real world around us. An example of a musical score influenced by "fractal ideology" is «L'escalier du diable» («The Devil's Staircase»), a fortepiano etude by modern composer Gyorgy Ligeti[17] . He, by the way, wrote that "direct transposition of fractal geometry into music is silly. I try to find music fractals by intuition …" His music begins with transparent and clear construction and step by step becomes more and more dynamic due to overlapping musical themes.

The fact that this etude has mathematical elements follows from the title, "Devil Staircase",

Cantor's "Devil Staircase" of the second order.

which coincides with the name of a special mathematical function with some specific (if not to say – weird) properties which are related to the so-called Cantor's set.

The notes of the beginning part of the etude are presented below.

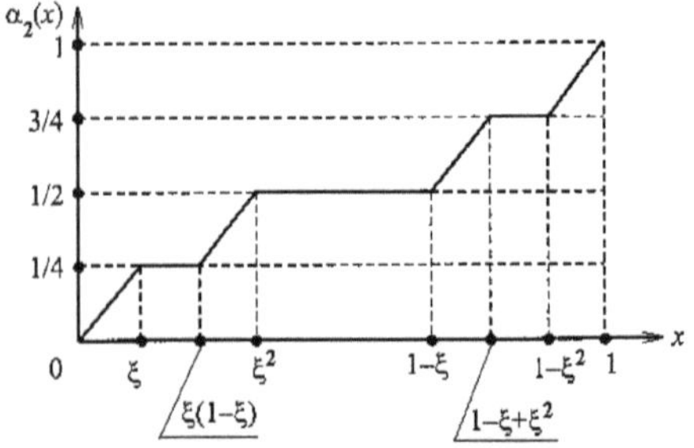

[17] **Gyorgy Sandor Ligeti** (1923-2006) was a modern Hungarian composer.

dédiée à Volker Banfield

Étude 13: L'escalier du diable

Auftragswerk des Süddeutschen Rundfunks Stuttgart für die Schwetzinger Konzerte

So we see that fractals, at least in concept, play a part not only in mathematics and physics but also in the entirety of human culture. And, if in previous times great scientists found inspiration in art and music, now painters and composers begin “to play on computers” to get inspiration…

2 UNUSUAL AND IMPOSSIBLE FIGURES

In a "topological Hell" we will write on Moebius' strips and drink from Klein's bottles...
Unknown author

2.1 Moebius Strip

Probably the very first unusual figure was invented by Moebius[18] in the middle of the 19th century. A Moebius Strip (or Moebius Band) is a simple and yet rather strange object.

Instead of presenting a formal definition, we show you below how to make a Moebius Strip.

The most amazing feature of this simple figure is that it has only one surface! If you take a sheet of paper, you can color each side of the paper with two different colors. If you try to color a Moebius strip, you find that you painted the entire surface with just one color, never having to lift your brush off the paper. Both sides of the strip – "inner" and "outer" – are colored with the same color!

[18] **August Ferdinand Moebius** (1790-1868), German mathematician and astronomer, who was a pioneer in the field of topology. Moebius, along with his better known contemporaries, Riemann and Lobachevsky created a non-Euclidean revolution in geometry.

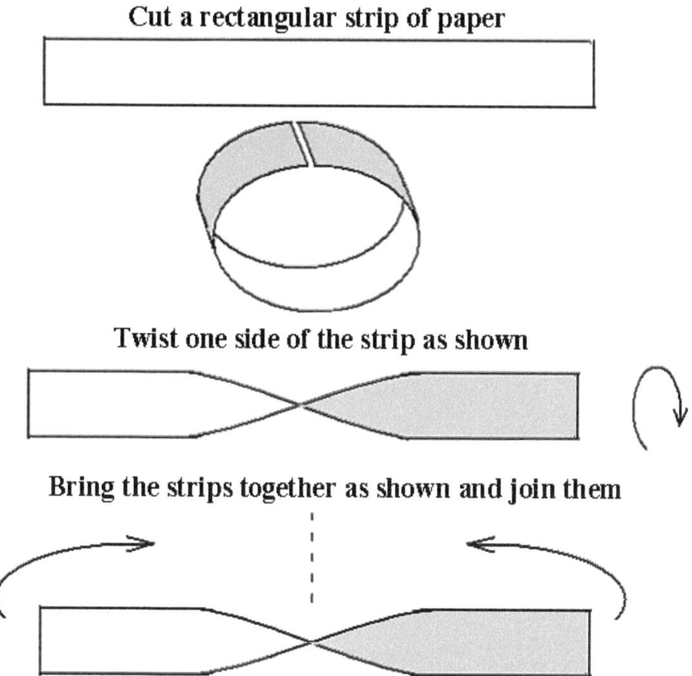

Rigorously speaking, of course, there is no "inner" or "outer" surface. Let's emphasize this point: Imagine a tiny creature running on the Moebius strip as if on a running track down the middle of the strip; it starts its run at some point.

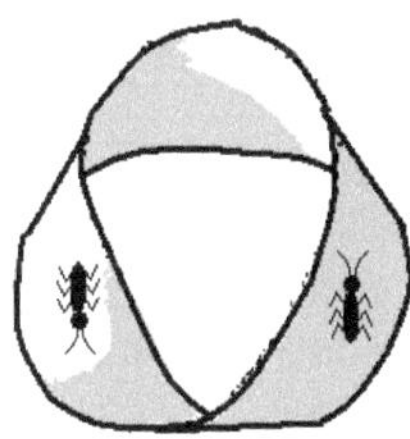

After going a distance equal to the length of the original strip it will find itself at a point exactly opposite, through the surface, of its starting point. And the creature will be able to run forever without encountering a boundary.

Escher's[19] painting, shown below, is a fun illustration of such a run.

[19] **Maurits Cornelius Escher** (1898-1972) was a contemporary Holland painter and graphic artist, founder of a new direction in graphic.

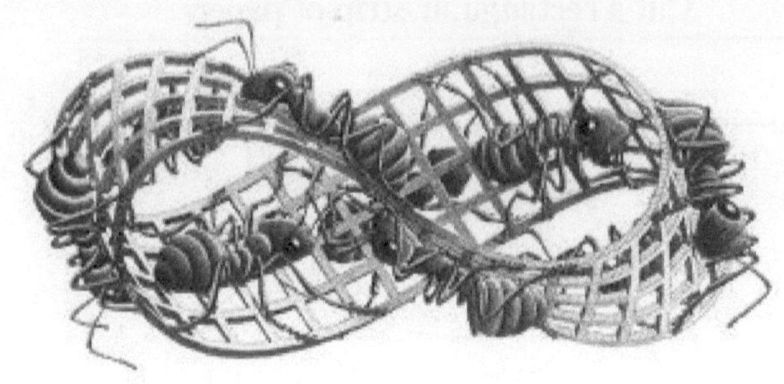

2.2 Let us play with Moebius strip!

Let us consider interesting metamorphosis that can be done with a "classical" Moebius strip. Make such a strip of wide piece of paper and cut it through the central line as it shown on the figure below. When you finish this you will see … again a Moebius strip but more "twisted" (see the right figure).

If an "Escher's ant" begins to run and travelling on both sides of the strip and at last returns to the start position.

A duble twisted Moebius strip

By the way, magicians who cut a simple Moebius strip in circus, call a double twisted Moebius strip as "Afghan strip". (It is clear that if one cuts in the same way just a simple ring, there will be two separated narrow rings.)

However, do not think that magic transformations with a Moebius strip are finished. What can we get if twisted a strip several times before fixing it in a close figure?

One can see on the figure below that in simplest cases, there will be a simple ring (no twist at all) and an ordinary Moebius strip.

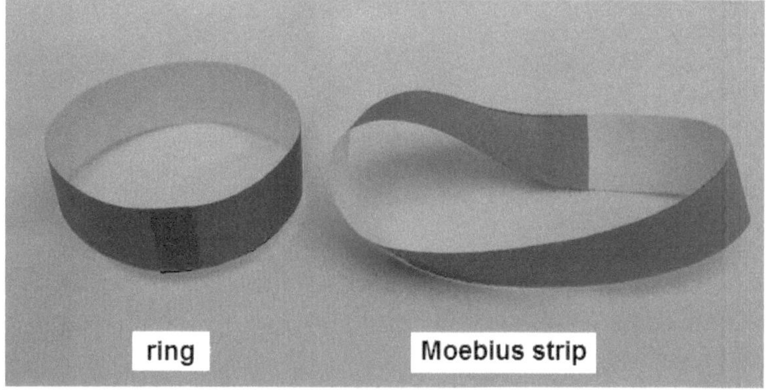

If one twists an initial strip twice, there will be a ring though "screwed": if an Escher's ant" will run on one side, it will never appear on the second side of the ring. I an initial strip will be twisted three times, one gets an "Afghan strip".

Of course, a stripe can be twisted repeatedly. If it will be twisted odd times (i.e. on angle $(2n+1)\times180^{o}$), we get a multiply "screwed"

Moebius strip, and it will be twisted even times (i.e. on angle $2n\times180^{\circ}$), we get a multiply "screwed" ring.

By the way, if one makes a chain using simple rings, an Escher's ant an run on inner face of one of the rings and on the outer face of the other ring. However, if a chain will be made from Moebius strips, the ant can reach any point on both faces.

One can continue to play with a Moebius strip. Let us take a wide strip and cut it as shown on the figure below. Then we can construct a "multi-level" Moebius strip!

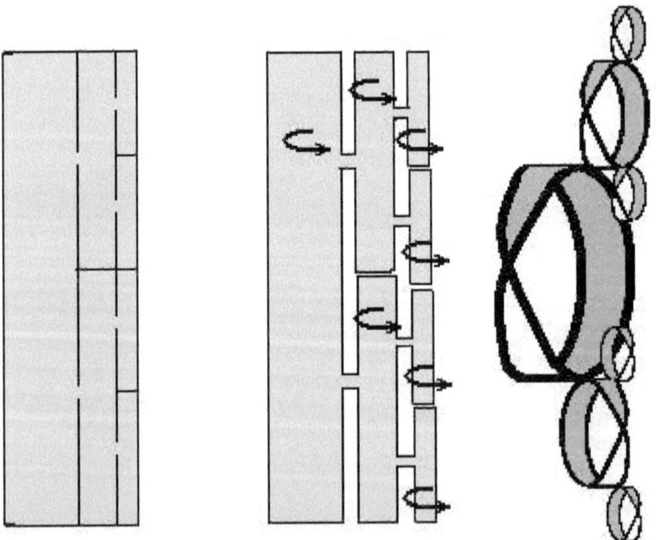

Of course, it is schematic picture. In reality, this figure looks much queerer.

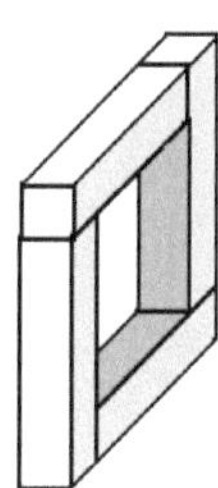

Could you imagine what an exciting travel can do an ant running on such "Moebius bush"?

At last, we can present a hole-ridden ring that possesses a property of a Moebius strip.

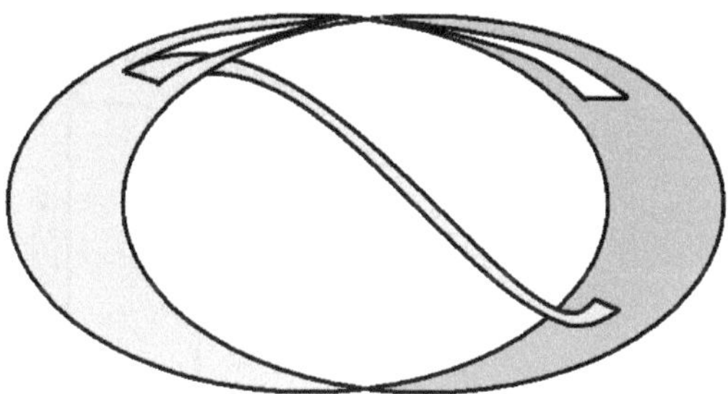

2.3 Moebius "frames".

Now take a frame with square cross-section. Make such a frame from four bars of plasticine.

What happens if we twist one of the bars on 90°, and then use it for constructing a frame?

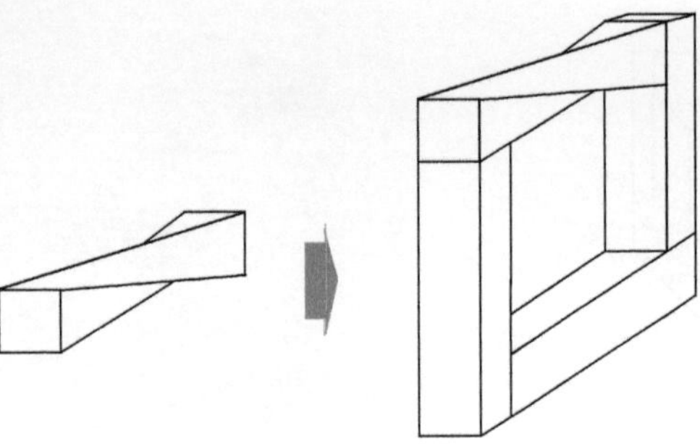

Now let us take a long paper strip and attach it to this "screwed" frame sit runs all sides in order. The order of the strip sequential attaching is shown below. If you wish it can be considered as a path that an Escher's ant is running.

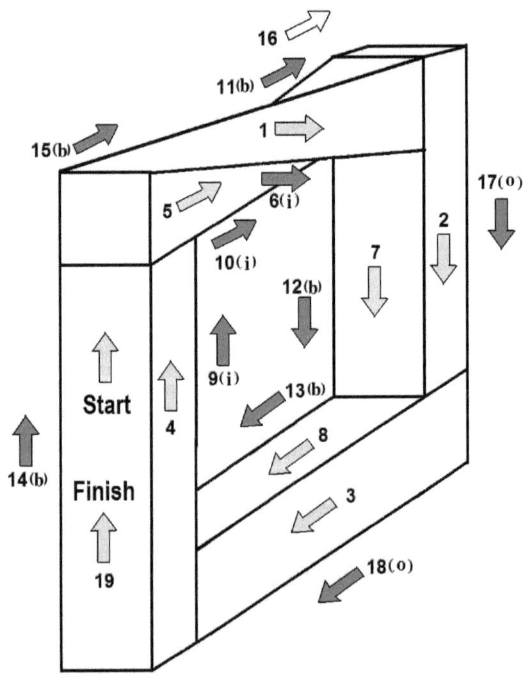

On the figure, light grey arrows denote visible sides and dark grey ones do invisible. Numbers correspond to the order of "travelling". Letters in braces denote a path on the invisible sides: (b) for back, (i) for inner and (o) for outer.

As you guess, the strip on the frames faces forms a "screwed" ring, not a Moebius strip: an Escher ant is running always on the same surface of the strip.

An what happens if a bar is twisted on 180°, not 90°? The procedure of making a double twisted bar is demonstrated on the figure below.

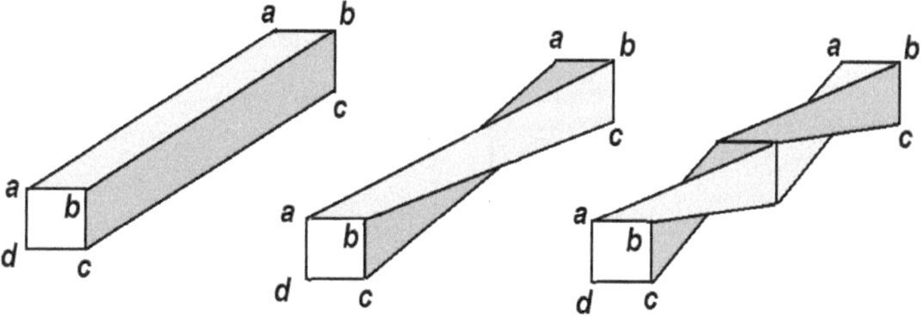

Assume that we twisted twice the same upper bar. In result we get the following frame:

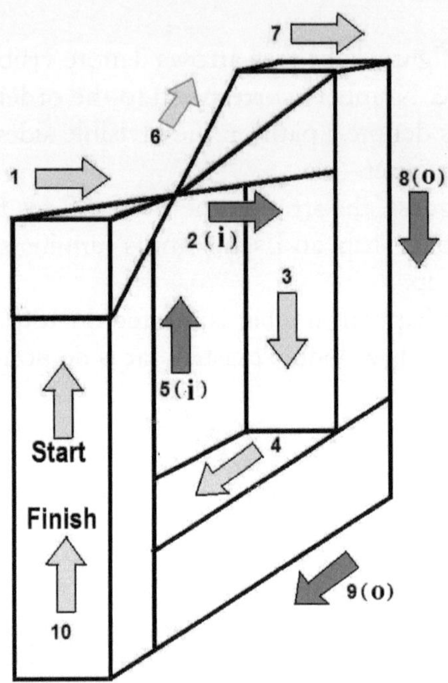

If an Escher ant starts and run over bar's sides, it will travel only on eight sides and return to the starting point. The strip putting on the ant's path forms a double "screwed" ring that include eight corresponding sides.

If an ant will start to travel from a neighbor side, it will run on other eight sides, i.e. in this case the frame could be covered by two double screwed rings.

What happens if the upper side is twisted on 90° clockwise and another one (for example the lower) anticlockwise on the same 90°? It is clear that the second twist compensates the first one and in this case there will be four simple rings, as it was with a simple non-deformed frame.

Of course, one can continue analogous exercises with bars that have different cross-faces in the form of regular polygons.

Actually, for investigating properties of twisted frames it is enough to consider hoops with corresponding cross-faces. It is easy enough to find that the number of rings formed by strips covering an "ants paths" will depend on the number of polygon vertices and the number of twists.

For example, consider a bar with a hexagon cross-face and make a single twist on $360^o/6 = 60^o$.

Afterwards, make a hoop and cover it with a strip. In result we obtain a single ring that is "screwed" 6 times.

If we twist the bar twice, i.e. on $360^o/3 = 120^o$, there will be two separated double twisted rings. After twist on 189°, there will be three simple rings.

One can observe that number 6 has the following simple dividers: 1, 2 and 3. In this the explanation lays why in this particular case we have one, two or three separated rings for corresponding cases.

In general, if a cross-face of a bar is N-sided polygon and N can be divided without remainder by numbers $K_1, K_2, \ldots, K_n$, then it is possible to get N/ K_1 rings with K_1 times "screwed" sides, or to get N/ K_2 rings with K_2 times "screwed" sides, or … to get N/ K_n rings with K_n times "screwed" sides.

At the end, look at figures taken from Gershon Elber's Internet site

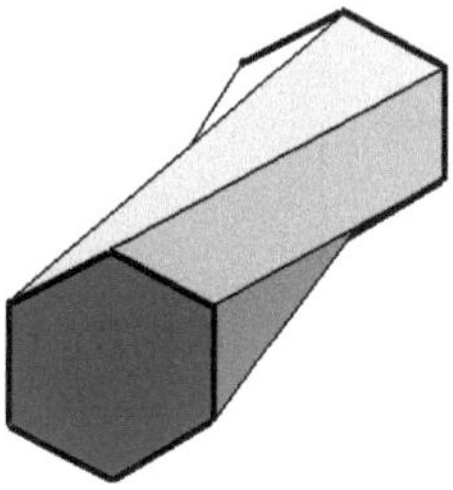

http://www.cs.technion.ac.il/~gershon/EscherForReal/ [20] .

[20] Published with the author's permission.

As usual, somebody could ask: "So what?!"

Nothing… Just interesting!

(By the way, nobody asked Moebius why he described his fancy strip ☺.)

2.4 Klein Bottle

About 20-30 years after this, Klein[21] invented the so-called Klein Bottle.

This bottle is the closed three dimensional analog of the two dimensional M?bius strip. Imagine that a funnel in the bottom of the bottle transforms into a hollow handle, which in turn, transforms into the bottleneck. You can imagine how a fly enters into the funnel, then goes to the inner surface of the handle and then appears upside down on the same point from where it made its entry. (One understands that this body has no "inner" or "outer" surfaces!)

[21] **Felix Christian Klein** (1849-1925) was a German mathematician who is best known for his work in non-Euclidean geometry, for his work on the connections between geometry and group theory, and for results in function theory.

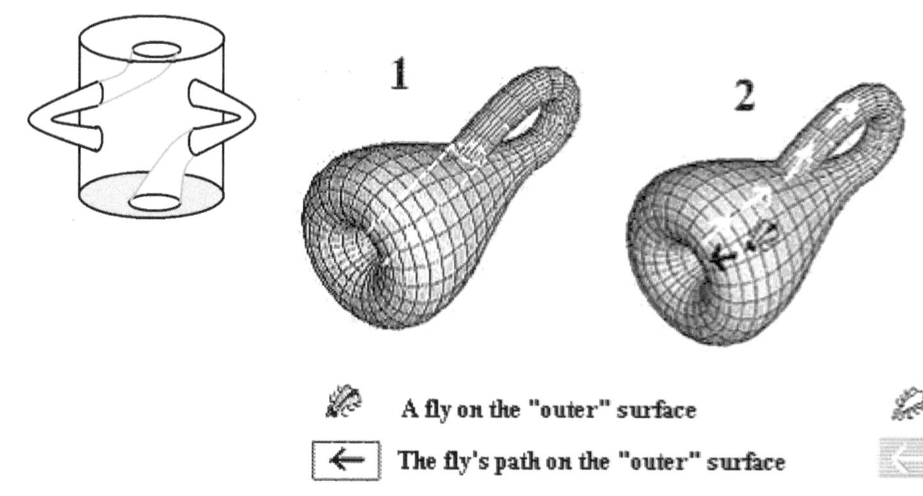

2.5. Infinitely Enclosed Klein "Mug"

> Mathematics is a single symphony of infinity'
>
> ***David Hilbert.***

To consider some interesting constructions concerning a Klein bottle, I was forced to introduce it in a non-traditional form – as a Klein "mug", which possesses all properties of Klein bottle but gives a possibility to demonstrate some transforms more visibly.

As you remember an "ant" can travel on a Moebius strip infinitely, moving always forward. In case of Klein bottle, an "ant" actually went in a "dead-end": it enters the bottle trough the bottle's handle and returned at the starting point by the same path. I decided to make such a Klein "mug" that an "ant" can return to the starting point, moving only forward. As a result, the Klein "mug" with "hole-ridden bottom": this mug has two symmetrical funnels at the top and at the bottom.

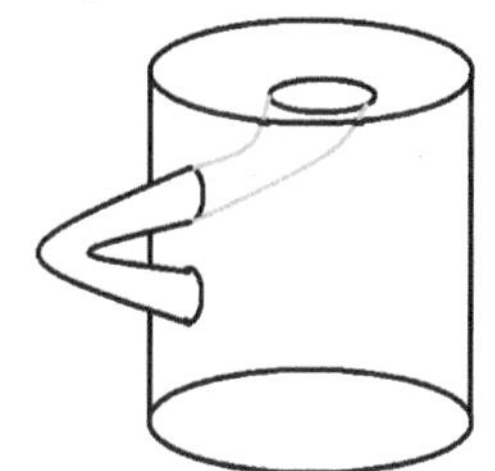

So, if you wish, appears Klein-Moebius bottle (or mug)!

By the way, why this mug is with a “hole-ridden bottom”? Let us pour liquid in the upper funnel. As soon as the liquid level arises up to the hole of the second handle, liquid begins to pour out of the mug!

And what if we embed a smaller mug into a large one?

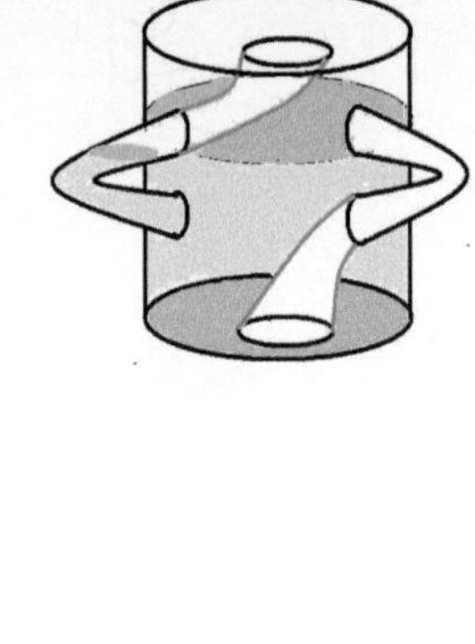

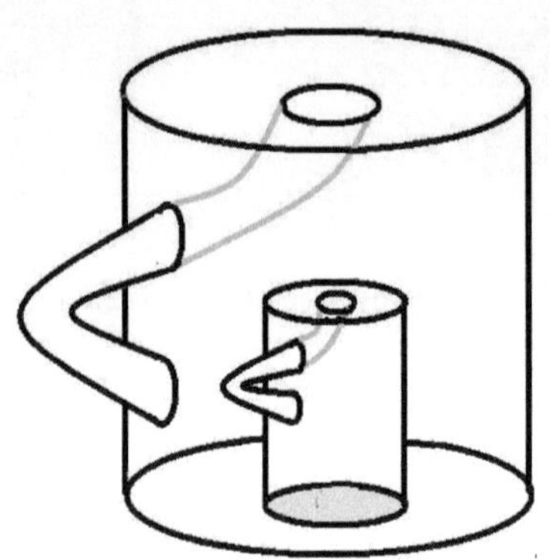

Of course, this embedded mug also can be done with a “hole-ridden bottom”.

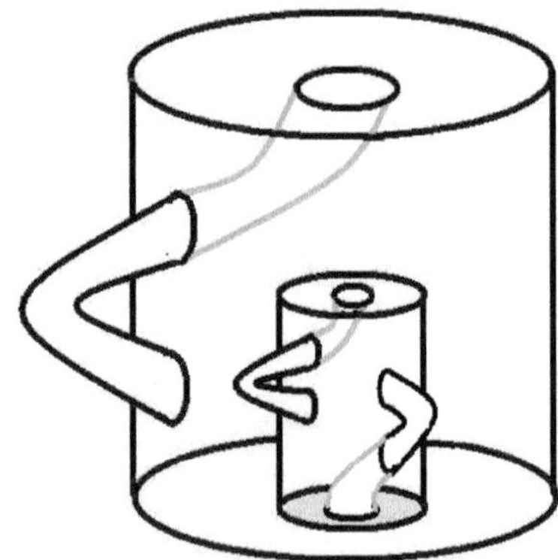

It is interesting that even with two embedded mugs there are two possibilities to “travel” inside them. Here is the second variant when an “ant” first enters a smaller mug and after this appears inside the larger one. Of course, there is a new variant for a hole-ridden bottom.

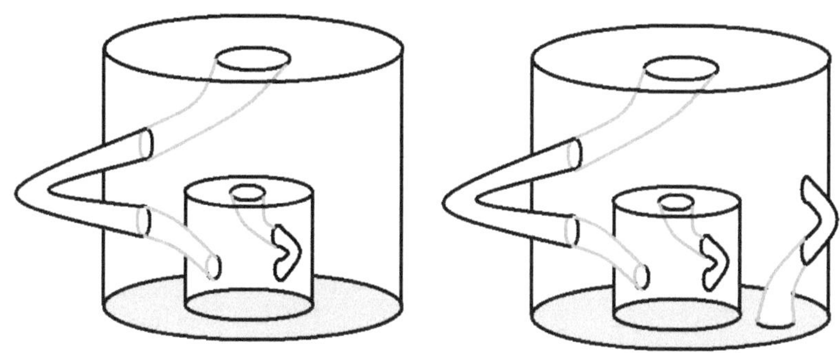

Further, we can easily construct three embedded mugs with the order of travel Big mug → Middle mug → Small mug.

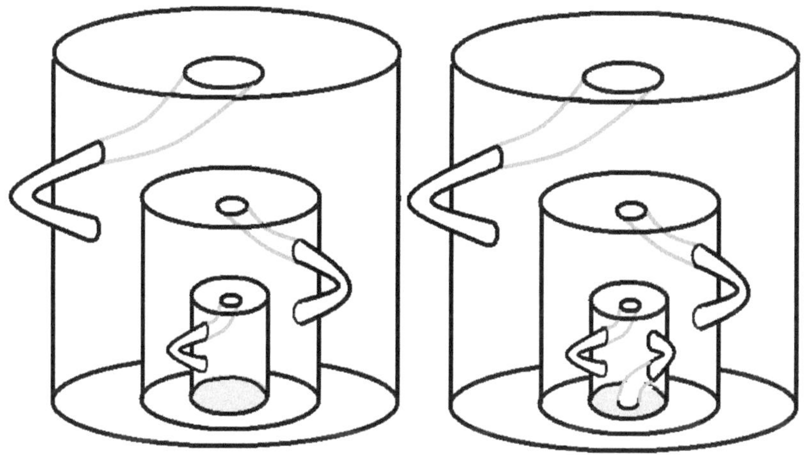

Of course, one easily can construct (at least mentally) arbitrary number embedded mugs, using a recurrent procedure explained on the figure below.

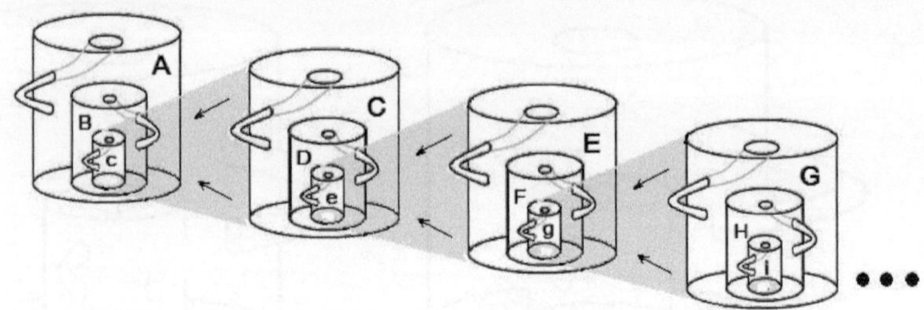

Interesting to notice that with increasing the number of embedded mugs the number of different travelling paths is also increases. For example, for three embedded mugs there are the following paths:

Enter → Big mug → Middle mug → Small mug,
Enter → Big mug → Small mug → Middle mug,
Enter →Middle mug → Big mug → Small mug,
Enter → Middle mug → Small mug →Big mug,
Enter → Small mug → Big mug → Middle mug,
Enter → Small mug → Middle mug → Big mug.

We present only the last variant. Others can be built in analogous way.

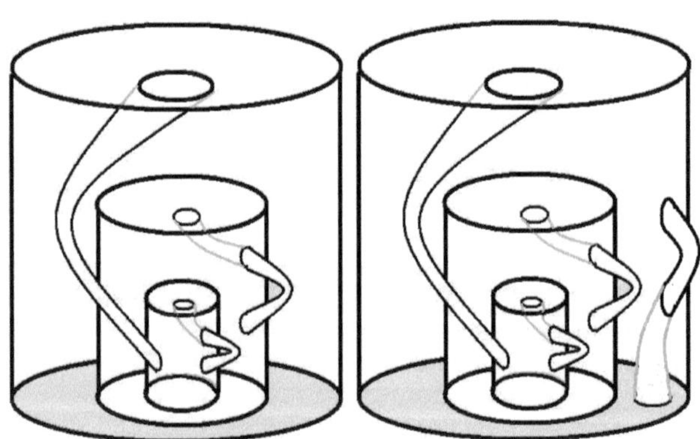

In other words, for *N* embedded Klein mugs there are *N*! different travelling paths depending on the order of connections of one mug with another..

You can try play yourself with various constructions consisting of Klein mugs: complex chains of mugs, branching systems of mugs, etc.

For instance, there is such funny "two storey" mug..

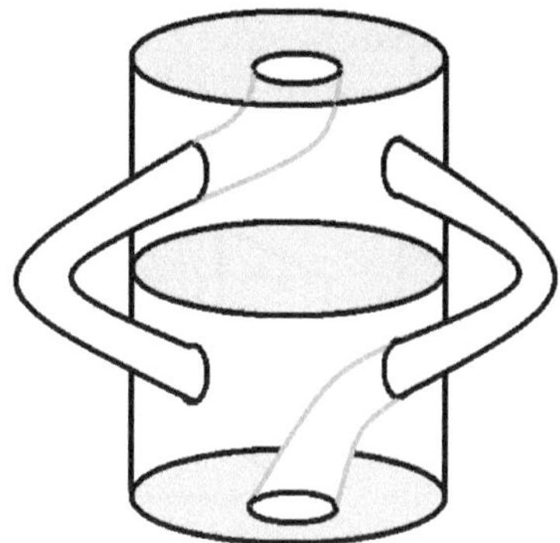

Again the same sacramental question arises: "So what?!" And again the answer is: "Nothing… Just interesting!"

2.5 Impossible Figures

However, while a Moebius strip and Klein bottle are real objects, impossible figures are quite a different case, like ghosts who exist only on the paper…

The very first impossible figure, a "cube," is attributed to Necker[22] . In 1832 he published pictures of an unusual cube that appeared to assume different orientations as one continued to look at it. This widely known illusion is reproduced below. Necker's cube is an ambiguous line drawing. The cube is presented in isometric perspective, which means that parallel edges of the cube are drawn as parallel lines in the picture. When two lines cross, one cannot understand which line is in front and which is behind. Namely this fact makes the picture ambiguous; the

[22] **Louis Albert Necker** (1786-1861) was a Swiss crystallographer and geologist

picture can be interpreted in two different ways. If we stare at the picture long enough, it will often seem to flip back and forth between the two valid interpretations (so-called multi-stable perception). Indeed, look at the pictures below where cubes with transparent sides are presented. Two first cubes have bold lines on the "visible" edges and thin lines for edges "visible" through the transparent sides. To offer some help in seeing the effects, we include small images of the same cubes, but with non-transparent sides.

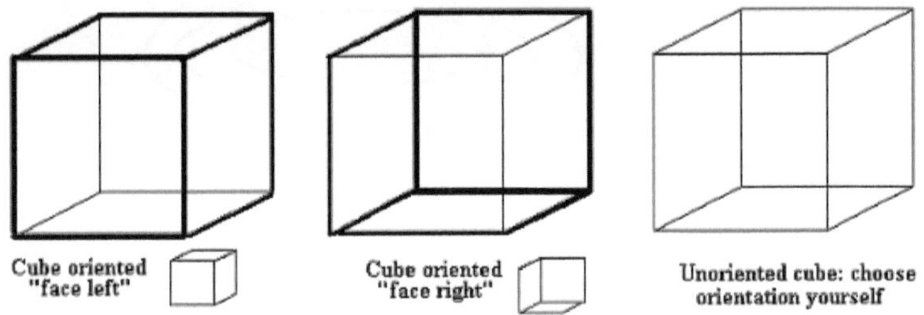

On the basis of this ambiguous cube, Necker's cube (which also is known as Escher's cube) was constructed.

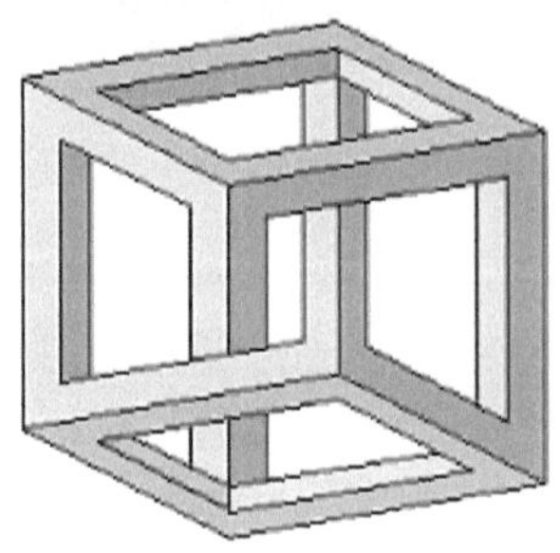

It took about a century, before in 1934 Swedish graphic artist Reutersward[23] created the first "impossible triangle," which is represented by a series of cubes.

An impossible figure fever was born! Reutersward created hundreds of various impossible figures. In 1980 the Swedish Postal

[23] **Oscar Reutersward** (1915-2002) was a Swedish graphic artist who is called as the father of impossible figures.

Service issued a series of stamps with some impossible Reutersward's figures (the leftmost stamp depicts an "impossible triangle").

Many graphic artists tried to invent impossible figures, however only Reutersward was successful in opening a new world of fantasy. Below are some of these figures:

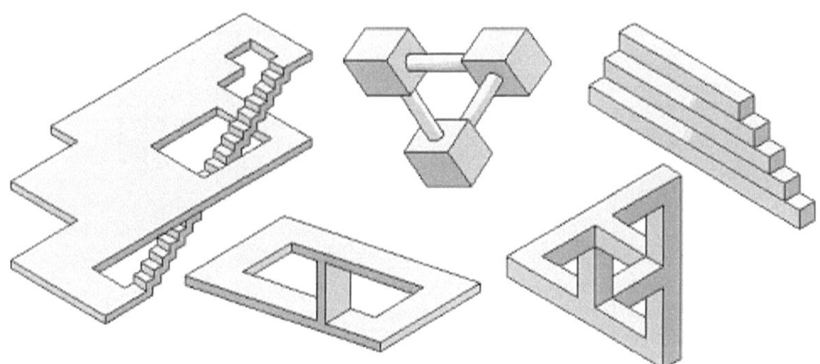

Meanwhile creating new impossible figures became the rage; painters to mathematicians and in between were creating those figures. Vlad Alexeev, a Russian graphic designer (see his website http://im-possible.info/), created some interesting figures.

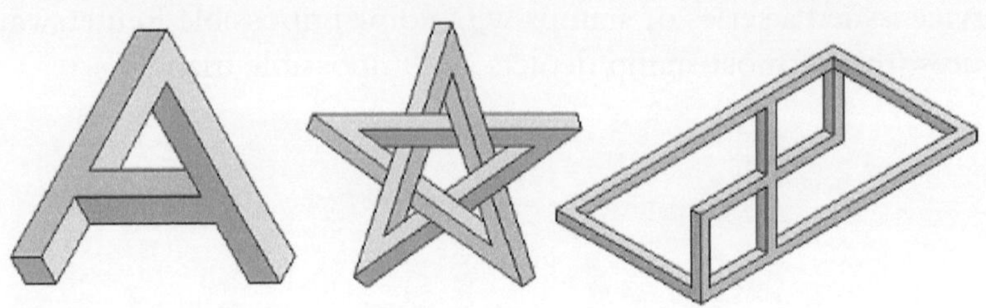

More samples of impossible figures created different graphic artists are presented below.

Then "impossible animals" began to appear: on the picture below there are dinosaurs, an elephant and a giraffe. (They are drawn with the usage of original ideas of V. Alexeev, P. Sheppard and A. Kravchenko , respectively.) Funny monsters, aren't they?

Let's close out this section of impossible figures with the figure below, which should remind you of a Moebius strip but it is not a Moebius strip; it is an impossible figure.

If you still find it difficult to recognize the figure as an impossible figure, look at this three-dimensional representation of a similar figure on the right.

Let us finish this section with a cartoon "on a Russian theme".

2.6 Mathematics and Fine Art

If nature were not beautiful, it would not be worth knowing, and if nature were not worth knowing, life would not be worth living.
H. Poincare[24]

Reutersward's inventions were notably original, but they were only interesting geometrical puzzles. However, as any interesting discovery, those works generated a new wave in drawing and graphics. The Dutch painter, Moritz Escher, started a revolution in modern graphic arts that is closely tied to mathematics.

Moritz Cornelius Escher
(1898-1971)

Holland painter, one of the most original graphic artists of modern times. He is known for his unusual drawing with impossible figures and ornaments, which cover the surface of a picture with various subjects without empty space.

Everything began with a curious incident. In the 1950s the English mathematician Penrose[25], who was interested in graphics and fine art, attended one of Escher's lectures. He was so impressed by the lecture that it influenced him to reinvent an impossible triangle based on Reutersward's work. He represented this figure in a "more usual" form (see the figure in the middle, below) than that by Reutersward (see the

[24] **Joules Henri Poincare** (1789-1857) was a French mathematician and physicist whom his contemporaries called "the first authority of the time". He left his mark in mathematics, physics and mechanics. He formulated the principles of special relativity theory before A. Einstein.
[25] **Roger Penrose** (born in 1931) is an English mathematical physicist.

figure on the left). In addition, Penrose invented a "closed staircase" that allows infinite ascending or descending – whether you ascend or descend depends on your subjective "feelings" (see the figure on the right).

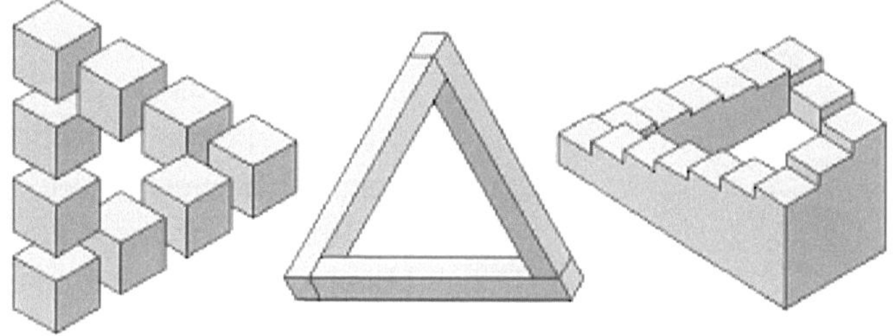

Penrose wrote a mathematical paper in which he presented his impossible figures. He sent the paper to Escher who was highly impressed by those pictures and subsequently used the "impossible staircase" in some of his drawings. Two expressive pictures by Escher using Penrose's staircase are presented below.

Belvedere

Waterfall

Impossible figures… Impossible figures…

Suddenly, you lose breathing: on Vlad Alekseev's site [26]you see a ***photo*** of Escher's "Belvedere"!

[26] http://im-possible.info/russian/articles/real/)

Definitely, photo of impossible figure needs special explanations… Otherwise, we should believe in supernatural things.

Let us begin with a simple example. Photo of impossible Penrose Frame has been done by a Holland teacher of physics and mathematics Hans de Rijk who used pseudonym Bruno Ernst.

On the same Vlad Alekseev's site there are explanations of how it was possible to make a photo of impossible figure.

On the first plan, one sees the "photo of impossible figure" and Same idea mirror reflection explains what is the "actual" impossible figure"! The problem is in a choice of angle of view.

Same effect was used with photo of Belvedere: the same figure under another angle looks quite different!

Talking about Escher's art would not be complete without mention of his detailed and masterful tessellations. His tessellations are made typically of images of living creatures which compactly cover a plane. Escher's interest in Oriental art led to his interest in tessellations. He traveled to Spain for the specific purpose of looking at Mauritanian ornaments made during the Arab Caliphate domain in the Pyrenees. He was impressed by the ability of Arab artists to fill ornaments with geometrical figures. One of Escher's famous sketches made in the Alhambra is shown below on the right.

Islam forbids painting images of living creatures (not only people, but animals, birds, fish as well), so Arab ornaments are composed only of geometrical figures. Escher decided to use in his ornaments and drawings living creatures.

Looking at this issue with a mathema-tical eye we note that there is a proof in geometry that a plane can be closely covered in a regular way only with triangles, squares and hexagons.

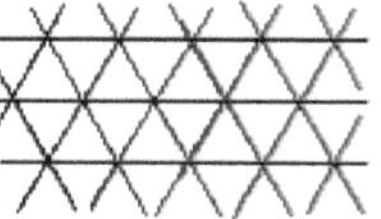

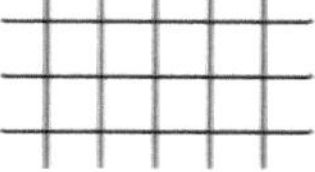

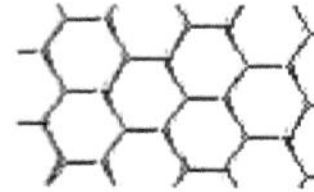

However, Escher showed that other compact coverings are possible with very fancy figures, for instance like these below.

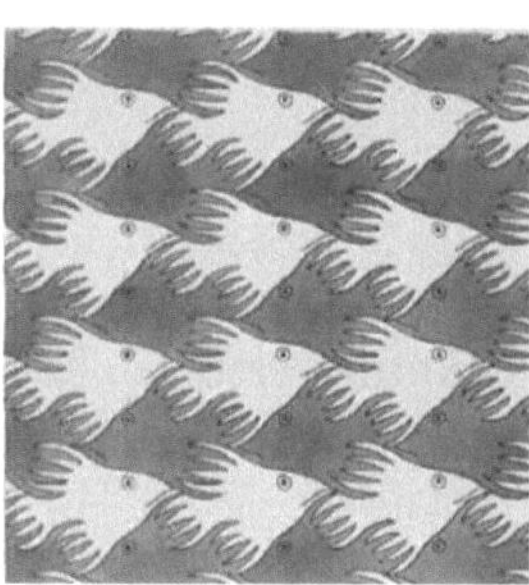

[27] Presentation of all pictures in this text has been permitted by Cordon Art's copyright department.

You can find out much more about Moritz Escher and his art at the Official M.C.Escher Website (http://www.mcescher.com/), published by the M.C. Escher Foundation and The M.C. Escher Company B.V. This website has also an extensive picture gallery there[27].

Mathematicians thus use Escher's works to challenge some of their theories. Escher's ornaments appear to be closely tied with the mathematical concept of periodicity and quasi-periodicity. Also, Escher's tessellations are applicable to the theory of crystallographic groups.

Ironically, Escher is not at all skilled in mathematics. Once he was invited to a lecture dedicated to the discussion of the mathematical content of Escher's own engravings and lithographs. To the mutual disappointment of both – the lecturer and Escher – the artist understood nothing... Later Escher wrote about this episode the following: "At school I never received a good mark in mathematics. It is very funny that now I begin to be associated with this discipline. Believe me, I was a very low level student at school. And now, mathematicians use my pictures in their books. Imagine, they greet me as a lost brother who has been newly found! It seems to me that they even don't suspect that in mathematics I am absolutely illiterate".

There are many books about this extraordinary artist. You can find numerous art albums with reproduction of his works. You can find information about Moritz Escher on http://www.mcescher.com/,that is running by the *Escher Foundation* and *The M.C. Escher Company B.V.* Here you find a gallery of Escher's works.

If you still never saw fantastic Escher's art, visit this site and you will get a real pleasure! There you can also buy beautiful reproductions and really fantastic art albums.

To conclude this section, look at Escher's beautiful etching, "Sky and Water."

3 "Golden Section"

> There are two treasures in geometry: they are Pythagoras' Theorem and the Golden Section. The first might be evaluated by a measure of gold and the second might be named a precious stone.
>
> ***Johannes Kepler***[28]

The Golden Section, also called the Golden Ratio or the Golden Mean is a unique way of dividing an interval into two pieces, such that the length of the larger part of the interval relates to the length of the smallest part as the length of the entire interval does to its largest part:

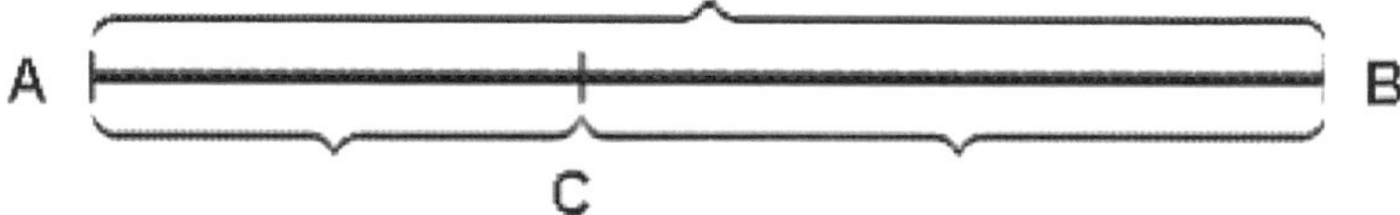

[28] **Johannes Kepler** (1571 –1630) was a German mathematician, astronomer and astrologer.

In other words, $\dfrac{AB}{CB} = \dfrac{CB}{AC}$.

3.1 History of the "Golden Section"

Euclid[29] in his "The Elements" already described dividing an interval in "extreme and mean ratio;" i.e. he talked about a "golden section" without giving to it a special name. The naming to "golden section" appeared only in medieval times.

Taking into account that $AB = AC + CB$ and the definition of our golden rule relationship, we do some simple algebra

$$x = \frac{AC + CB}{CB} = 1 + \frac{AC}{CB} = 1 + \frac{1}{\frac{CB}{AC}} = 1 + \frac{1}{x},$$

to get the following equation involving the golden ration, x:

$$x^2 = x + 1.$$

It follows that only the positive root τ has physical meaning:

$$x = \frac{1+\sqrt{5}}{2} \approx 1.618$$

Leonardo da Vinci coined the name "Golden Section", or "Golden Ratio." Maybe Leonardo was not the first who used this name because some believe that the term was used by Claudius Ptolemy[30], who used it while studying the proportions of a human body. Anyway, it was Leonardo da Vinci who popularized this.

Leonardo da Vinci

(1452 - 1519)

Genius Italian painter, sculptor, scientist, engineer

[29] ... C) was an ancient Greek mathematician, the author of the first ... s having come to our days. *In more details see Chapter "Pantheon" in* ...

[30] ... (85-165) was a great ancient Greek astronomer and geographer.

It is likely that ancient mathematicians also discovered the Golden Section while considering the so-called "neighboring squares" – a simple rectangle comprised of two squares.

The diagonal of such a rectangle with sides 1 and 2 (recall the Pythagorean Theorem) is equal to the $\sqrt{5}$. So, the value of $1+\sqrt{5}$, which is equal to the sum of a side of one of the squares plus the diagonal of the rectangle, is double the value of the Golden section. This is illustrated below:

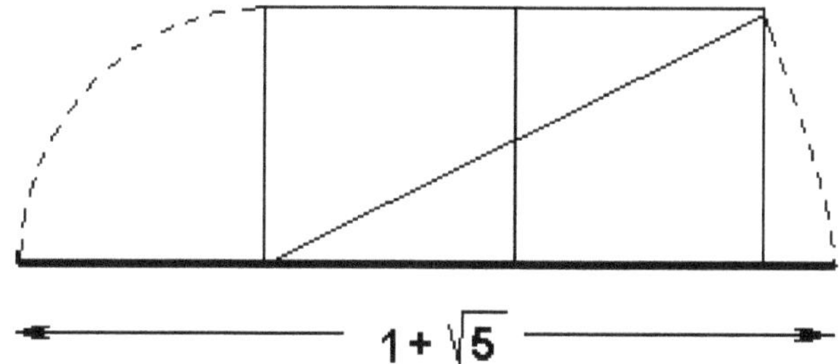

$1+\sqrt{5}$

(Details to show methods of construction of a Golden section are given in the next section, page 2.)

Let's rewrite our previous equation:

$$x^2 = x + 1,$$

in the form:

$$x = 1 + \frac{1}{x}.$$

It is interesting that for the value of x, one can construct an elegant chain fraction in the following way: Substitute for x in the denominator to form the following fraction:

$$x = 1 + \frac{1}{1 + \frac{1}{x}}$$

Continuing the procedure, one generates an infinite chain fraction of the kind:

$$x = 1 + \cfrac{1}{1 + \cfrac{1}{1 + \cfrac{1}{1 + \cfrac{1}{1 + \dots}}}}$$

One can get another interesting representation of x. Let us rewrite the equation $x^2 = x + 1$ in the form $x = \sqrt{x+1}$. Making substitution of x under the square root, one gets $x = \sqrt{1 + \sqrt{1 + x}}$, and then continuing the procedure infinitely, one gets a new representation of the Golden Section:

$$x = \sqrt{1 + \sqrt{1 + \sqrt{1 + \sqrt{1 + \dots}}}}$$

Evidently, the concept of the Golden Section was known to Pythagoras[31]. One can find a number of examples when ancient Greeks used the Golden Section in architecture. For instance, in the famous ancient temple, the Parthenon, one can find the systematic use of Golden Sections in the building construction.

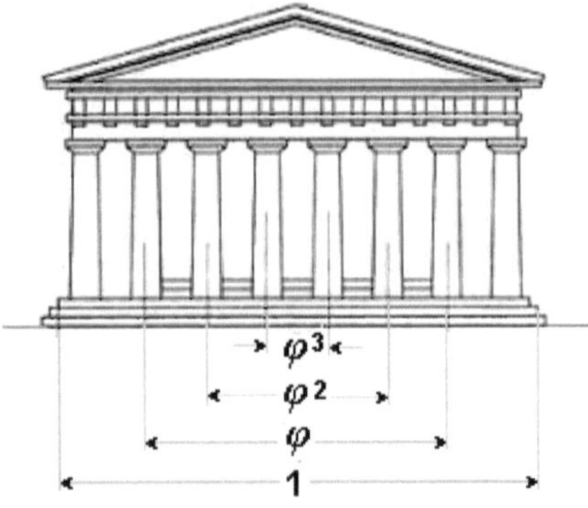

[31] **Pythagoras of Samos** (580 – 500BC) was a great ancient Greek philosopher, mathematician, astronomer and poet. Founder of religious-philosophical school (Pythagorean Brotherhood).

There is an hypothesis that the concept of this proportion arrived in Greece from ancient Egypt and Sumeria. Anyway, one can find this proportion in the Great Pyramid of Egypt – the pyramid of Khufu (also known as Cheops), which belongs to the Seven Wonders of the World. And notice that the pyramid was built in the third millennium BC!

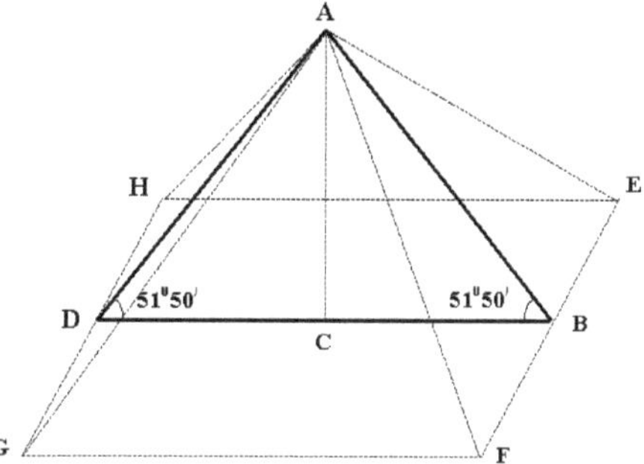

In Medieval Europe the Golden Section "came back" through translations from Arabic translations of Euclid's Greek originals. And it is interesting to notice that the "secrets" of the Golden Section were known only to a few people. Leonardo da Vinci widely used the Golden Section studying an "ideal human body." Due to him an interest in the Golden Section arose among scientists and artists.

Taken by the intriguing properties of the Golden Section, Leonardo started to write a book on geometry, but during this effort he found the book, «Divina proportione» ("Divine proportion"), by Luca Pacioli[32], that so impressed him that stopped working on his own book and instead created excellent illustrations for Pacioli's book. This book played a significant role in the science and art of those times.

> ***Remark***: Being a monk and a product of his time, Luca Pacioli found "Divine sense" in the Golden Section. He mentioned that it reflected the Divine Trinity: the small part personified the Son of God (i.e. Jesus Christ), the large part personified God and the entire interval personified the Holy Spirit. (At last, the Divine hierarchy was given a mathematical order!)

[32] **Fra Luca Bartolomeo de Pacioli**, or **Luca di Borgo** (1445–1514) was an Italian mathematician and Franciscan priest. Friend of Leonardo da Vinci.

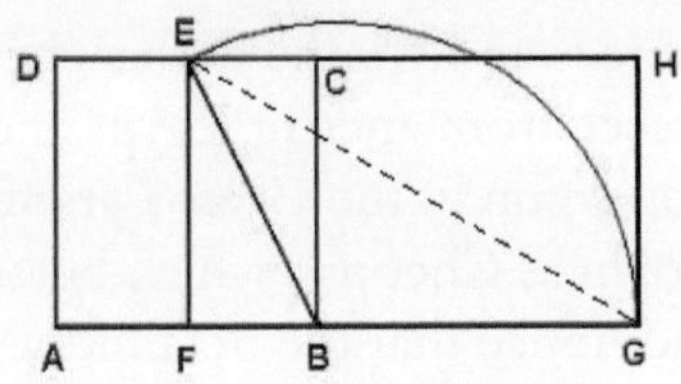

3.2 How to construct the Golden Section

We can easily construct a Golden Section with the help of dividers and a ruler. Let us divide an arbitrary interval AB into two equal parts: AO=OB. From point B draw a perpendicular and mark point C such that BC=OB. Connect Point C to point A, i.e. construct right triangular ABC. On the hypotenuse find point D such that *CD=BC,* and then find point *E* on *AB* such that *AD=AE.* The point (*E*) divides *AB* into a Golden Section, i.e. $\frac{AB}{AE}=\frac{AE}{EB}$.

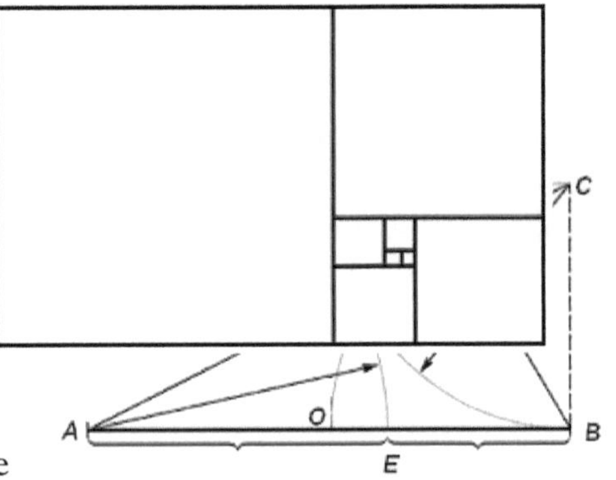

If the length of interval *AB* is taken equal 1, then the lengths of intervals *AE* and *BE* can be expressed by the infinite irrational decimal fractions *AE* = 0,618... and *BE* = 0,382... .

Another (equivalent) construction method of a Golden Section follows: Let us draw a square *ABCD.* Divide the square into two equal parts *AFED* and *FBCE.*

On the horizontal line find the point G such that BG= BE, where BE is a diagonal of the rectangle FBCE. By the Pythagorean Theorem, $BE=\sqrt{(FB)^2+(FE)^2}$. Let FB=1, then $BE=\sqrt{1^2+2^2}=\sqrt{5}$. Because triangles EFB and EFG are similar, it follows that $\frac{FB}{EF}=\frac{EF}{FG}$.

The constructed rectangle *EFHG* has lengths of a larger side to a smaller one relates as $\frac{FH}{EF} = \frac{1+\sqrt{5}}{2}$ and it is called the "Golden Rectangle".

The Golden Rectangle possesses an interesting property (by the way, as so do other geometrical figures belonging to the "golden family"): it is possible to construct an infinite sequence of embedded Golden Rectangles.

To find the intervals of the Golden Section, one can use a pentagon, i.e. a regular polygon. The word "pentagon" (in Greek "*penta*" means "five" and "*gon*" – "angle") is well known even to people far from geometry due to the name of the headquarters of the US Department of Defense, which is located in a building laid out in the form of a pentagon.

Recall Durer[33] from a previous section? He invented a simple rule for pentagon constructing, which is demonstrated below.

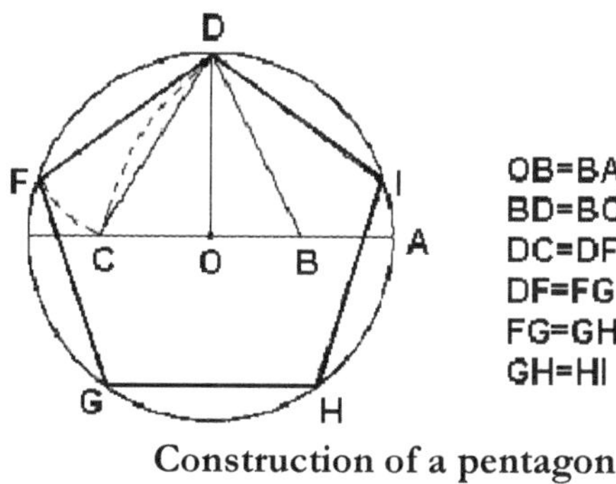

Construction of a pentagon.

[33] **Albrecht Durer** (1471-1528) was a German painter , wood carver, engraver and mathematician, one of the greatest masters of Western art in Renaissance.

The method is as follows: Draw a circle with the center at *O*. Take an arbitrary point *A* on the circle. Divide the radius *OA* into two equal parts so that *OB*=*BA*. Erect the perpendicular *OD* to the radius *OA*. Using dividers, find the point C on the diameter so that *BC* = *BD*. The length of a side of an inscribed pentagon is equal to *DC*. So if one marks the point F on the circle such that *DC*=*DF*, then the first side of the pentagon, *DF*, has been found. Further construction of the pentagon is extremely simple: From point *F* one finds point *G* on the circle such that *FG*=*DF*, and so on.

Connecting each vertex with the other ones produces a pentagram (in Greek "*gramma*" means "*line*"), i.e. regular five-pointed star. The pentagram itself consists of a smaller pentagon *FGHKL* in the center, with each side sporting an isosceles triangle. There are several Golden sections in this figure. For instance, segments *AF* and *FG*, *AB* and *BH*, *AE* and *EL* are golden sections.

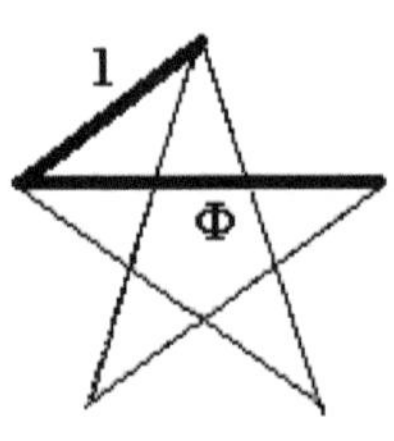

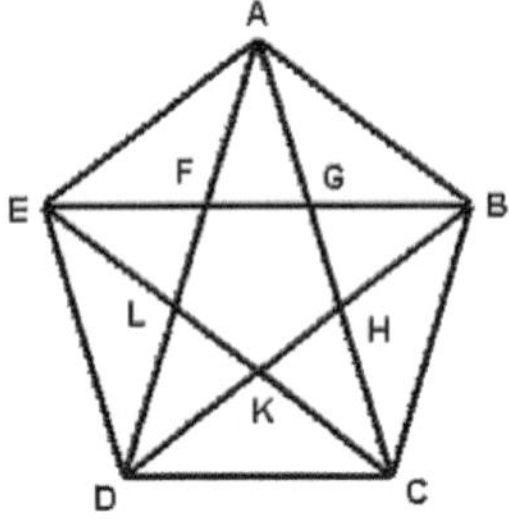

By the way, the longer segment of the paired two that make up a golden section is labeled in mathematics standard notation with the symbol Φ in honor of Leonardo Fibonacci, an Italian mathematician.

In ancient times, Pythagoreans already had noted that a new smaller pentagon could be constructed inside the inner pentagon and that this procedure could be continued infinitely. Thus a pentagon can be filled with infinite number of smaller and smaller pentagons.

The Pentagram was a special symbol among Pythagoreans. According to one legend, a dying Pythagorean being thankful to a man who took care of him yet having no money to pay him, asked the man to draw a pentagram on the door of his house. That kind man complied with the dying man's final request. Several years later someone from the Pythagorean brotherhood entered the house of the kind man, and, seeing the pentagram, generously rewarded the man.

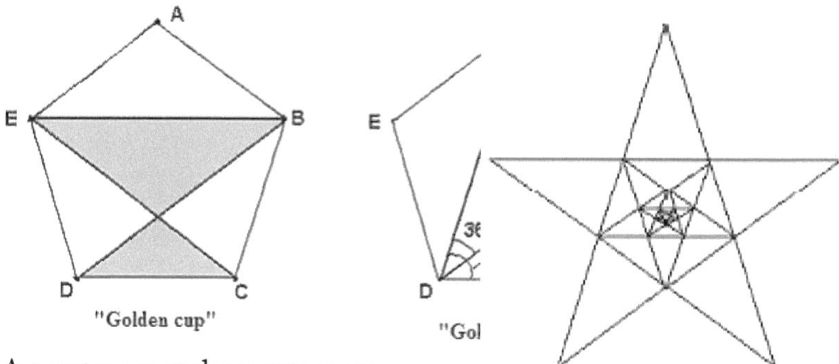

A pentagon and a pentagram include some worth mentioning figures that were widely used in ancient art, for instance, the so-called "Golden cup" and "Golden triangle", which are fragments of pentagram.

Each "Golden triangle" has an acute angle of 36° at the top and acute angles of 72° at the base (see triangle *ADC*). The ratio of a side to the base is a golden section. Bisector *DH* coincides with the diagonal, *DB*, of the pentagon and divides the side *AC* at point *H* into a golden section. The triangle *DHC* is a golden triangle. The bisector to angle *DHC* generates a new "Golden triangle," and so on. Pythagoreans saw something magic in the embedding of a figure inside a figure up to an infinite. Some interesting examples of embedding pentagrams are given below.

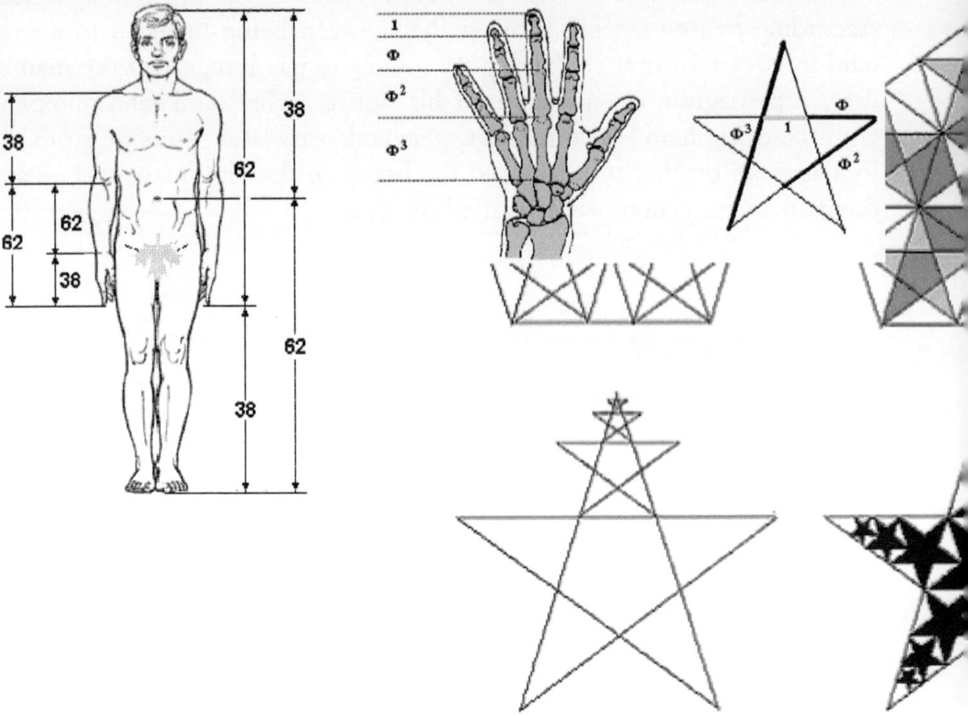

3.3 "Golden section" in Nature

The great German painter Albrecht Durer studied proportions of a human body. He found an important role of a "Golden section." Human height is divided at the waist into golden proportions; the bones of the middle fingers are in a golden proportion; the lower part of the face is divided in a golden proportion by the mouth; etc.

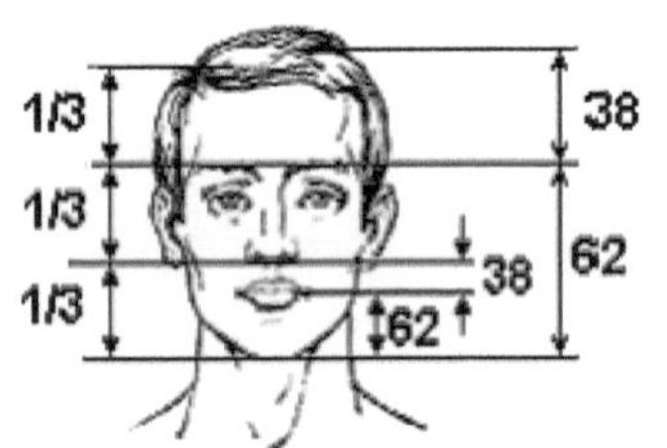

There are "Golden sections" in different fragments of a human palm.

The great astronomer of the 16th century Johannes Kepler[34] when he studied the growth of plants and their structures was the first who paid attention to the role of the "Golden section" in botany. Kepler called the Golden section "self-generating." "It is constructed in such a way, – wrote Kepler, – that any two members of this infinite chain being summed give a new member neighboring to the bigger one, and extraction of the smaller member from the larger one produces a new member that is neighbor to the smaller one of two previous; such procedure can be continued infinitely kin both sides".

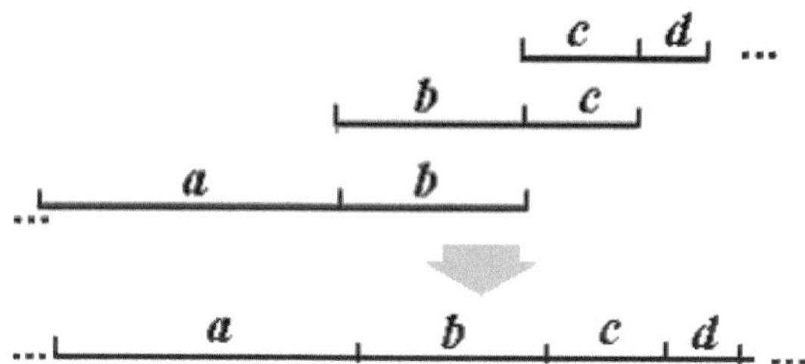

Indeed, since $a = b + c$, we get $a - b = c$; then from $c + d = b$ follows $d = b - c$, and so on.

Indeed, new branches of some plants form a sequence that is very close to the "Golden sections" sequence mentioned above. The main stem gives

---

[34] **Johannes Kepler** (1571-1639) was a great German astronomer, mathematician and naturalist, who was one of the founders of the modern naturalism. He is famous for his discovery of laws of planets' rotation.

the first branch at the distance *a* that grows up to some limited length. Then the second branch appears at smaller distance after the first one… Such development continues with the main stem and with its branches …

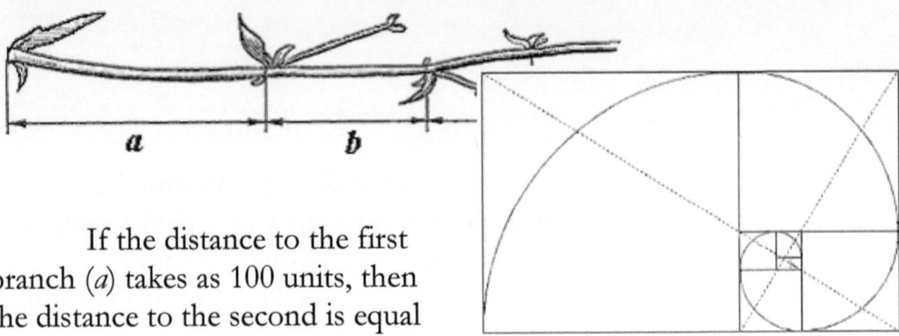

If the distance to the first branch (*a*) takes as 100 units, then the distance to the second is equal approximately 60-62 units, the distance to the third is about 38-40 units, the distance to the forth is about 24-25 units and so on.

A "Golden section" can be found in a bird egg.

Talk about "Golden sections" is incomplete without the mention of the "Golden spiral." A golden rectangle is a starting point for the construction of a golden spiral.

The golden rectangle ABCD first is divided into a square AEFD and the smaller golden rectangle EBCF. Then the rectangle EBCF is divided into a square EBHG and the golden rectangle GHCF, and so on. This process can be continued infinitely. The embedded golden rectangles have a point of attraction located on the intersection of the diagonals of the all embedded golden rectangles. Drawing segments of circles within each square, one can construct the "Golden spiral."

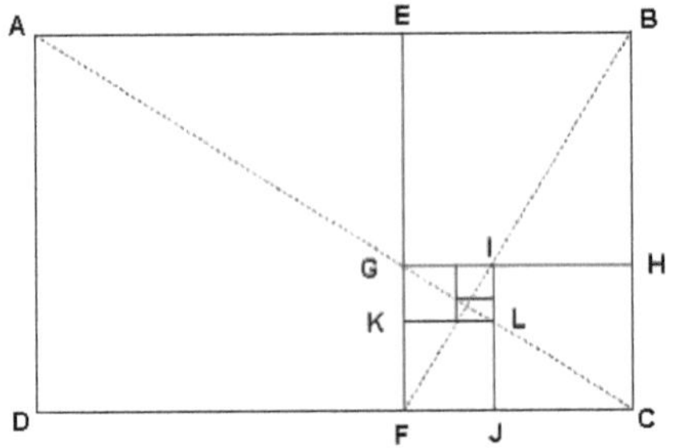

A "Golden spiral" is a variant of the so-called logarithmic spiral. From each point of this spiral one can move inside to the point of attraction or outside, going to infinity.

In nature such spirals are common; some examples are: the tail of a comet, the horns of some animals, and the already mentioned mollusk shells.

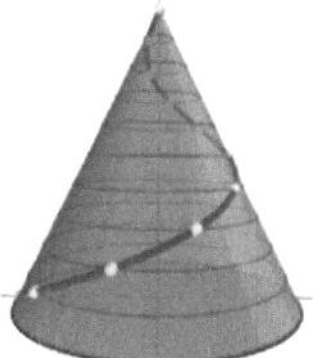

Archimedes[35] was interested in the nature of a spiral and discovered the equation for a spiral. The spiral corresponding to his equation is called an "Archimedes' spiral".

3.4 "Golden section" in art

Painters and sculptors subconsciously, just being led by their

[35] **Archimedes** (287–212 BC) was the greatest a… …an and physicist.

intuition, use the golden sections regularly. In most paintings by classical artists a central figure is placed from the frame edges at a distance that matches golden proportions. It may be noted that artists of the Renaissance did it almost always intentionally because of their knowledge of the laws of art.

Let us consider one of the most famous paintings in the world – Leonardo da Vinci's Mona Lisa, which also is known as La Gioconda (or La Joconde). This portrait was painted in accordance with the proportions of a golden triangle.

Another one of Leonardo's well-known works is his fresco, "The Last Supper," which also is based on the proportions of a golden section.

One can find golden proportions in many pictures of landscapes. For instance, in the picture, "The evening bell ringing," by Russian painter Isaak Levitan[36], the horizon divides the vertical in a Golden proportion.

[36] **Isaac Ilyich Levitan** (1860-1900) was a classical Russian landscape painter who advanced the genre of the "mood landscape".

In another picture by Russian painter Shishkin[37], "A forest of ship timber" the nearest pines divide the picture into a Golden section horizontally

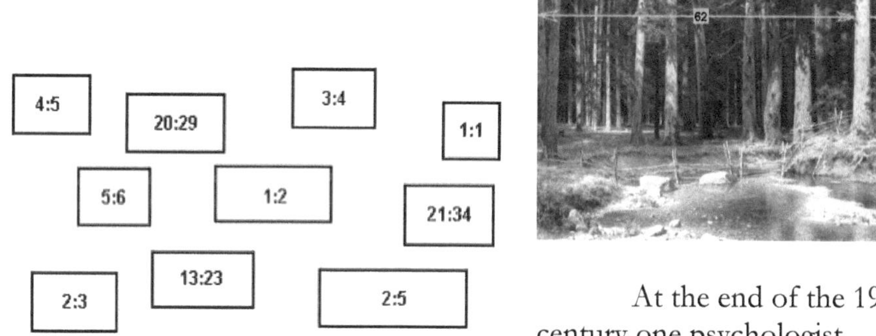

At the end of the 19th century one psychologist performed a test checking "the feeling of beauty" among adults. About five hundred people (men and women in about equal proportion) were given a set of ten rectangles from which they were to choose the one they

---

[37] **Ivan Ivanovich Shishkin** (1832- 1898) was a Russian landscape painter.

liked best. Those rectangles had proportions of sides from 1:1 to 2:5. The criterion was qualitative: "Which form is more pleasant for your eye?" One of the rectangles, with a ratio of sides equal to 21:34 ($\approx$0.6765) was practically the golden rectangle. About 35% of all 500 people chose the golden rectangle, the second and third places with about 20-25% of the vote was for rectangles with sides ratio 2:3 ($\approx$0.6667) and 20:29 ($\approx$0.6897), approximating the golden rectangle...

That experiment showed that, indeed, there are some proportions that are "more pleasant to the eyes."

The "Golden section" came into printing as well. Albrecht Durer wrote a book about the construction of Latin letters in which he widely used squares and golden rectangles. Some examples of the letters designed by Durer are shown below.

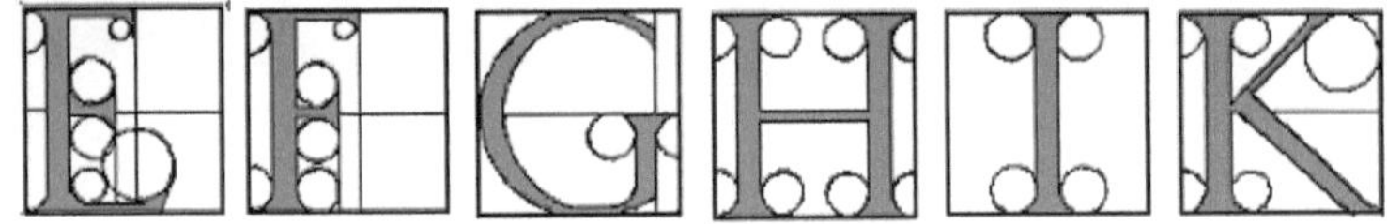

3.5 Fibonacci numbers

The name of Italian mathematician Leonardo Fibonacci is associated with the "Golden section" in a very intriguing way. His famous book, "The Book of Calculations" ("Liber Abaci", or "The Book of Abacus[38]"), contains the following problem: "A man puts a pair of

Leonardo Fibonacci
(1170-1250)

One of the most outstanding mathematicians of the European Medieval. His influence on development

wooden computer" in the world, which is still widely used in Asia.
out 2000 BC in China and Babylon. "*Abacus*" means "*calculation*" in

mathematics with the so-called Fibonacci numbers.

baby rabbits into an enclosed garden. Assuming each pair of rabbits, upon reaching two months of age, produces a new pair every month, the new pair from the second month on itself becoming productive. How many pairs of rabbits will there be in the garden after one year?"

Thus, in the beginning of the first and second months there is a single pair of rabbits, i.e. the beginning of the Fibonacci sequence is {1, 1}. At the end of the second month, there are two pairs of rabbits: the initial one and a new one, so the sequence on the second step of the process has the form: {1, 1, 2}. Next month, the elder rabbits produce one more pair, though a young pair does not, so at the beginning of the 4th month the sequence is {1, 1, 2, 3}. Now two pair of rabbits are productive, so at the beginning of the 5th month the sequence of Fibonacci numbers is {1, 1, 2, 3, 5}, and so on.

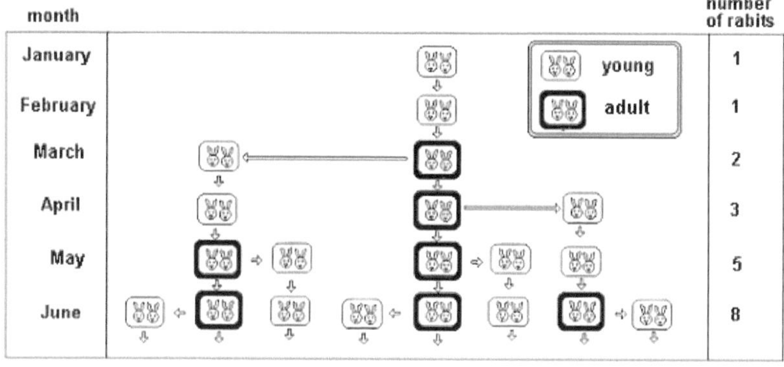

In 100 months the number of pairs of rabbits becomes astronomical: 354 224 848 179 261 915 075.

The process of rabbit reproduction can be described as follows: Let us denote by F_n the number of pairs of rabbits after n months. The number of pairs after $n + 1$ months, F_{n+1}, is equal to the number of pairs at the n-th month, i.e. F_n, plus the number of newborn pairs. The number of pairs of mature rabbits at that moment is equal to F_{n-1}. Thus the following equation can be written:

$$F_{n+1} = F_n + F_{n-1},$$

With initial conditions: $F_0 = 0$ and $F_1 = 1$ one gets the following numerical sequence: 0, 1, 1, 2, 3, 5, 8 ... which bears the name of Fibonacci numbers.

Well, it is fair to ask where the golden section is in all this. To answer this question, let us consider the ratio $F_n : F_{n+1}$. The beginning of the set of these values is given in the table below.

№	F_n	$F_n : F_{n+1}$
0	0	0
1	1	1.000000
2	1	0.500000
3	2	0.666667
4	3	0.600000
5	5	0.625000
6	8	0.615385
7	13	0.619048
8	21	0.617647
9	34	0.618182
10	55	0.6179775
11	89	0.6180556
...	...	...

It is easy to see that the ratio $F_n : F_{n+1}$ converges to the "Golden section" with increasing n.

Notice that the same limit of the sequence will be obtained if one takes other initial conditions. For instance, let us take $F_0=3$ and $F_1=-1$. A new table of $F_n : F_{n+1}$ ratios for these initial conditions is presented below.

№	F_n	$F_n : F_{n+1}$
0	3	-3
1	-1	-0.5
2	2	2
3	1	0.333333
4	3	0.75
5	4	0.571429
6	7	0.636364
7	11	0.611111

8	18	0.62069
9	29	0.617021
10	47	0.618421
11	76	0.617886
...	...	...

As one can see from the new table, the convergence of the sequence to the golden proportion is kept even under the new initial conditions. The difference at the 14th step is only in the 5th decimal! O course, that this happens is easily explained because moving forward, the initial conditions become unimportant in the sequence.

Fibonacci did not investigate the mathematical properties of the sequence he had obtained: 1, 1, 2, 3, 5, 8, 13, 21, 34, 55, 89 ... This was done by other mathematicians. Since the beginning of the 19th century, mathematical works dedicated to the development of Fibonacci sequence – as was said by one sharp-witted mathematician – "began reproducing like Fibonacci rabbits." Probably, the most work on this subject was by the French mathematician Lucas[39]. By the way, it was he who coined the name "Fibonacci numbers" and also introduced the so-called generalized Fibonacci numbers which are described by the following recursive formula:

$$G_n = G_{n-1} + G_{n-2}.$$

Depending on initial G_1 and G_2 this recursive formula generates infinitely many Fibonacci type numerical sequences. Among them the most significant applications has been the so-called Luca's numbers, L_n, that are defined as the following recursive equation:

$$L_n = L_{n-1} + L_{n-2}.$$

With initial conditions of $L_1 = 1$ and $L_2 = 2$. The sequence of the Luca's numbers has the form: 1, 3, 4, 7, 11, 18, 29, 47, 76, 123, 199... .

Usually, one considers Fibonacci numbers, F_n, and Luca's numbers, Ln, for the cases for which the subscripts n are natural: 1, 2, 3, ...

[39] **Francois Eduard Anatole Lucas** (1842-1891)was a French mathematician. The most important works had been done in the number theory and indefinite analysis. He developed the method of selecting Mersenne's primes.

. However, it is interesting that these sequences make sense even for negative numbers n: –1, –2, –3.... These new sequences were called "expanded sequences" These expanded Fibonacci and Luca's numbers are presented in the table below.

n	0	1	2	3	4	5	6	7	8	9	...
F_n	0	1	1	2	3	5	8	13	21	34	...
F_{-n}	0	1	-1	2	-3	5	-8	13	-21	34	...
L_n	2	1	3	4	7	11	18	29	47	76	...
L_{-n}	2	-1	3	-4	7	-11	18	-29	47	-76	...

From the table, one can observe that terms of the sequences of F_n and L_n possess some interesting mathematical properties. For instance, all odd $n = 2k + 1$ terms of sequences of F_n and F_{-n} coincide, i.e. $F_{2k+1} = F_{-2k-1}$, and for even $n = 2k$ they are different in their signs, i.e.: $F_{2k} = -F_{-2k}$. The opposite situation is observed with Luca's numbers, L_n, i.e. $L_{2k} = L_{-2k}$ and $L_{2k+1} = -L_{-2k-1}$.

Looking at the table in more detail, one can find the following relationships between Fibonacci and Lucas' numbers:

$L_n = F_{n-1} + F_{n+1}$, where n can be equal to 0, ±1, ±2, ±3...

Indeed, for instance, Lucas' number $L_4 = 7$ is equal to sum of two following Fibonacci numbers: $F_3 = 2$ and $F_5 = 5$.

For curious readers, let us notice that Fibonacci and Luca's numbers have a number of other interesting relations, for instance:

$$F_{n-1} \times F_{n+1} = F_{n-1}^2, \text{ if } n \text{ is even, and } F_{n-1} \times F_{n+1} = F_{n+1}^2, \text{ if } n \text{ is odd,}$$

$$\text{i.e. } F_n^2 - F_{n-1} \times F_{n+1} = (-1)^{n+1};$$

$$L_n = F_n + 2F_{n-1};$$

$$L_n + F_n = 2F_{n+1}.$$

Thus, Fibonacci numbers possess a number of interesting properties. As we have already mentioned, ratio $F_n: F_{n+1}$ with $n \rightarrow \infty$ converges to 0.618034..., i.e. to the number Φ, and the ratio $F_n: F_{n-1}$, naturally, converges to 1.618034... . The ratio of two Fibonacci numbers $F_N: F_{n+2}$, converges to 0.381966... , that is the inverse of 2.618034... , that is, in turn, the ratio $F_n : F_{n-2}$.

The number Φ is the only number which when incremented by 1 produces its own inverse[40], i.e.: $0.618+1=\frac{1}{0.618}$. Such properties of Φ allow writing the following set of equalities:

$0.618^2 = 1 - 0.618$,
$0.618^3 = 0.618 - 0.618^2$,
$0.618^4 = 0.618^2 - 0.618^3$,
$0.618^5 = 0.618^3 - 0.618^4$, and so on.

In an analogous way:

$1.618^2 = 1 + 1.618$,
$1.618^3 = 1.618 + 1.618^2$,
$1.618^4 = 1.618^2 + 1.618^3$,
$1.618^5 = 1.618^3 + 1.618^4$, and so on.

It is possible also to write the following interesting equalities:

1) $1.618 - 0.618 = 1$,
2) $1.618 \times 0.618 = 1$,
3) $1 - 0.618 = 0.382$,
4) $0.618 \times 0.618 = 0.382$,
5) $2.618 - 1.618 = 1$,
6) $2.618 \times 0.382 = 1$,
7) $2.618 \times 0.618 = 1.618$,
8) $1.618 \times 1.618 = 2.618$.

There are other interesting properties of Fibonacci numbers. For instance, if any of Fibonacci number (except 1 and 2) is multiplied by 4,

[40] From this point, we will use numbers with only 3 decimals. It is done only from the clarity viewpoint.

then there exists a Fibonacci number such that when added to this product produces a Fibonacci number. For instance:

$3 \times 4 = 12$; if add to this Fibonacci number 1, then $12+1= 13$,
$5 \times 4 = 20$; if add to this Fibonacci' number 1, then $20 + 1 = 21$,
$8 \times 4 = 32$; if add to this Fibonacci number 2, then $32+ 2 = 34$,
$13 \times 4 = 52$; if add to this Fibonacci number 3, then $52+ 3 = 55$,
$21 \times 4 = 84$; if add to this Fibonacci number 5, then $84+ 5 = 89$, and so on.

4 Pythagorean Geometry

Let no one inapt to geometry come in
Inscription over the door
of Plato's Academia

4.1 Pythagoras' Theorem

"Theorem" is a Greek word that in antiquity meant any show dedicated to gods, such as sports, theater, solemn parades, etc. ("Theo" in Greek is "god".) The first discoveries by ancient geometers seemed to the Greeks to be so significant as to warrant being called "theorems." Let us consider as an example one of such theorems proved by Pythagoreans, who were disciples and followers of great Pythagoras:

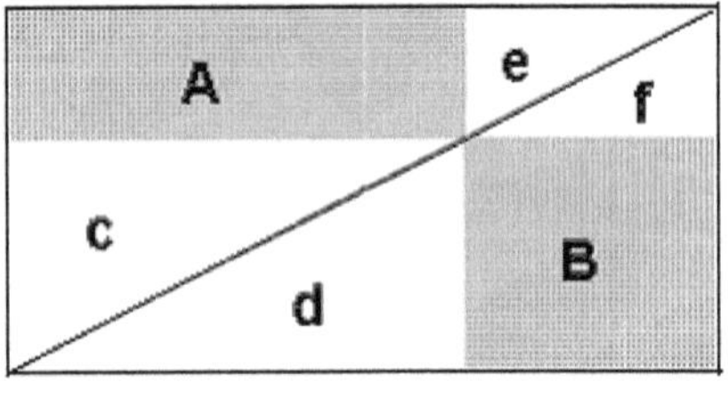

If one takes an arbitrary point on the diagonal of a rectangle and draws two lines each of which is parallel to one of the rectangle's side, then the two rectangles that appear on both sides of the diagonal have equal areas.

The proof of such theorems in Pythagoras' school usually came to down to a single phrase, "See the drawing." We use the same method though we supply hints such as: by construction $A+c+e=B+d+f$, and $c=d$ as well as $e=f$. How simple and how elegant!

Probably it is appropriate to mention here a joking definition of "axiom" attributed to Euclid[41]: *If nobody can prove a statement to be a theorem, then it becomes an axiom.*

Pythagoras of Samos

(580 - 500 BC).

One of the greatest founders in science. Mathematicians, astronomers, philosophers, biologists and many others consider him as one of the founders of their sciences. Many maxims from his "Golden Verses" became proverbs in many languages of the World. At the end of the 6th century BC, he created a scientific brotherhood of Pythagoreans that successfully operated during tens of years after his death. That scientific school produced a number of outstanding philosophers, historians and mathematicians.

For more details see Chapter "Pantheon".

By legend, Pythagoras of Samos[42] is the author of the famous theorem that bears his name. There is even a proof that is ascribed to Pythagoras himself.

The Pythagorean Theorem states the following:

For any right triangle the
square of the hypotenuse is equal to

[41] **Euclid** (365-300 BC) was a great ancient Greek mathematician, the author of the very first tractates on mathematics.

[42] To the name of great mathematician Pythagoras one often adds "of Samos" to distinguish him from another Pythagoras who was a sculptor in the 5th century BC. That Pythagoras was born in the city of Regia and is called Pythagoras of Regia.

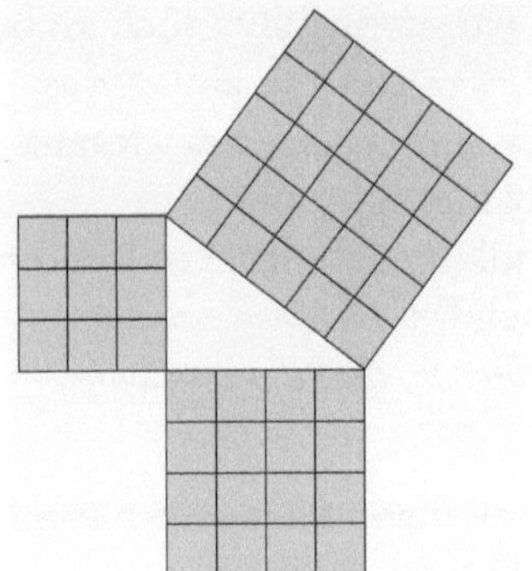

the sum of the squares of the two sides.

This wondrous property of right triangles was known before Pythagoras, though it was known only for some particular cases. Just direct measurements show that a right-angled triangle with sides equal to 3 and 4 units has a diagonal equal to 5 units.

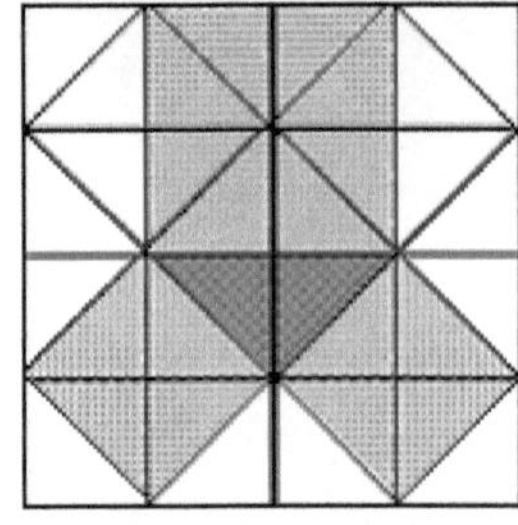

This triangle (3, 4, 5) was known by ancient Egyptian land surveyors and architects; they knew that the areas of squares built on the sides are equal to 9 and 16 units, and the area of the square built on the diagonal is equal to 25 units (9 + 16 = 25).

The simplest "visual proof" of the Pythagorean Theorem is for an isosceles. Probably, the proof of the theorem began from here. Really, it is enough to look at the drawing to be convinced of the correctness of the theorem: 8 small triangles form two squares built on the sides of the central darker triangle, and 8 triangles form the square built on the hypotenuse of the central triangle.

By the way, such a drawing is found in many ancient manuscripts.

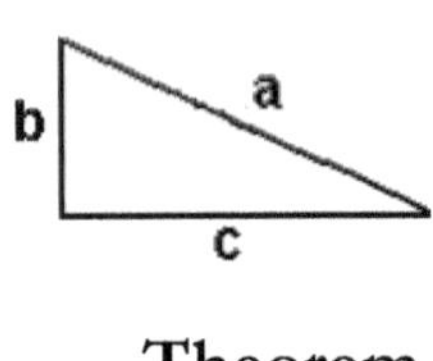

4.2 The Proof of the Pythagoras' Theorem

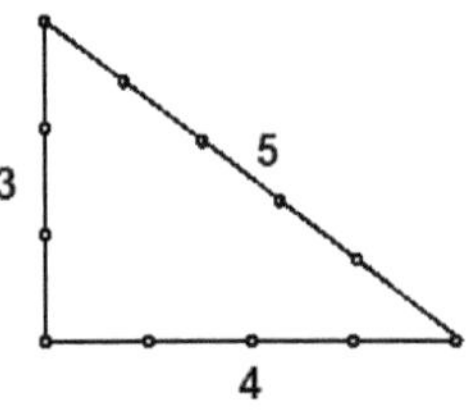

Let us consider the proof that by legend is attributed to the greatest ancient mathematician himself. Let us consider a right triangle.

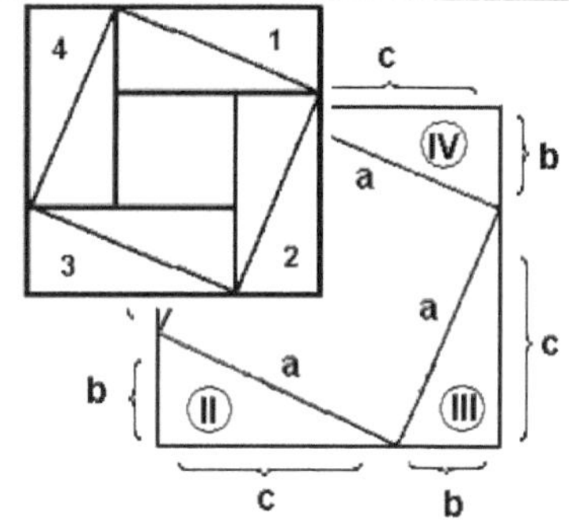

Build a square with a side equal to the sum of sides *b* and *c* of the original triangle.

Now divide this square into two squares b2 and c2 and two equal rectangles with sides b and c by drawing corresponding lines as shown in the diagram. In turn, divide these two rectangles into four equal right triangles I, II, II and IV. The area of each of them is equal to bc/2, i.e. the area of all four of them is equal to 2bc. From here it follows that the square with a side b+c after extracting on area 2bc is equal to b2+c2. Now in the same larger square with the side a + b locate the same four triangles I, II, II and IV in a way shown on the next drawing. It is easy to see that inside we have a square with the side equal to the triangle's hypotenuse.

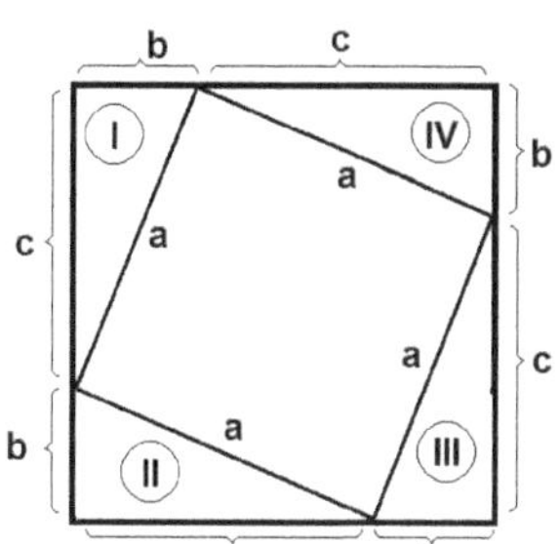

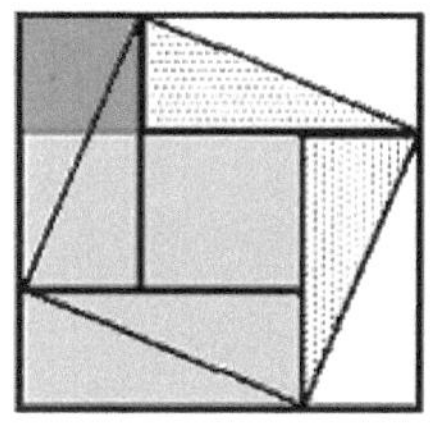

If now we again exclude from the larger square the area equal to $2bc$, then the remaining area is equal to a^2. Thus we have proved (actually, Pythagoras had proved) that $a^2 = b^2+c^2$.

* * *

In principle an analogous proof was obtained in ancient China. Consider again a larger square with sides equal to $b+c$.

It is clear that if one excludes triangles 1, 2, 3 and 4, then the remaining square is one with a side equal to a. Now let us build from the fragments of the larger square a figure that was called "a bride's chair".

The shadowed part of the picture looks like a chair, and with some imagination one can see

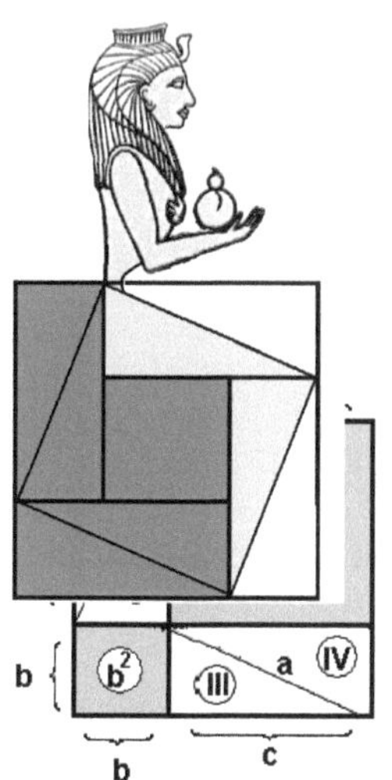

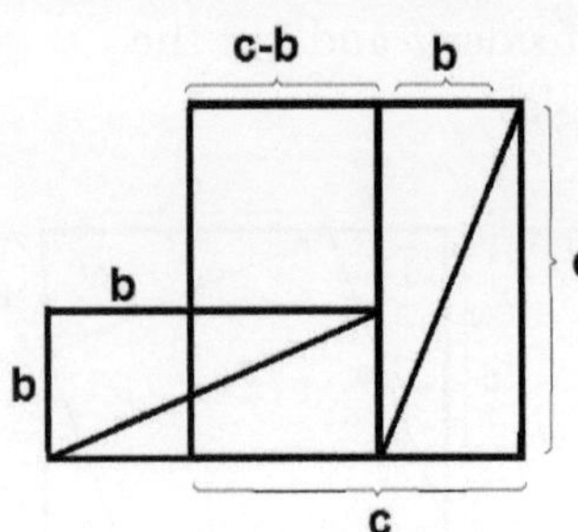

that somebody is sitting on the chair (if you accept a cubist Picasso style of painting)...

This "chair" consists of two squares, one with side *b*, and another with side *c*. Thus, if one excludes the four non-shadowed triangles, then the remaining area equals b^2+c^2, proving that $a^2=b^2+c^2$.

Indian mathematician Bhaskara[43] in one of his manuscripts made the drawing below and annotated it with a truly Pythagorean comment, "See the chart!"

Let us note that there are about 400 various proofs of the Pythagorean Theorem, including one by Garfield[44], the President of the USA.

[43] **Bhaskara Achārya** (1114-1185) was an Indian mathematician-astronomer.
[44] **James Abram Garfield** (1831-1881) was the 20-th President of the USA who was killed in 4 months after inauguration (doubtlessly not for the Pythagoras Theorem proof ☺).

PANTHEON

Pythagoras of Samos

(580 - 500 BC)

Pythagoras is one of the greatest scientists of all times. Mathematicians, astronomers, physicists, biologists, philosophers and many others consider him to be the founder of their sciences.

Although Pyth*a*
Samos often is hailed a
pure mathematician an
indisputably is one of t
greatest figures in ancient Greece, remarkably little is known of l
and specific works. The code of secrecy that marked the Pythag
brotherhood may be largely responsible for this unfortunate lack
records.

Pythagoras was born on Samos, an island in the Aegean Sea. Mnesarchus, his father, a merchant from Tyre, was granted citizenship in Samos in acknowledgment and gratitude for his delivery of wheat to Samos during a famine. Pythais, his mother, was a native of Samos. Pythagoras' name, according to some sources, means "*forecasted by Pythia*;" he was given this name to acknowledge the Pythia[45], who foretold his birth and predicted his wisdom. However, it seems more reasonable to

[45] The Pythia was the priestess at Apollo's oracle in Delphi. (The name comes from Python, the dragon that was slain by Apollo.) The Pythia operated as a vehicle for Apollo's will to be known to those on earth.

assume the more prosaic hypothesis that Mnesarchus named his son after his beloved wife, Pythais.

The main source of information about Pythagoras comes from Iamblichus'[46] work, which was written many centuries after Pythagoras. Little is known of Pythagoras' childhood, however, it was said that he was well educated in music and poetry. He was physically healthy and once he won a "boxing match" at one of the first Olympic Games. There is an entertaining claim that referees initially did not want to allow him to participate because of his short height.

As a youth, Pythagoras probably was a pupil of Pherecydes[47] in Lesbos, and a pupil of Thales[48] and of his pupil Anaximander[49] in Miletus. These three famous philosophers evidently influenced Pythagoras' interests in geometry and cosmology.

In about 535 BC Pythagoras, apparently in response to Pherecydes' or Thales' advice, Pythagoras went to Egypt, where he spent about 20 years with the priests of Memphis, Heliopolis and Diopolis. While in Egypt he studied geometry, about which he likely already was acquainted given his studies with Thales and Anaximander. When Egypt was conquered by Persia, Pythagoras was taken to Babylon and held as a prisoner for twelve years. By one account, he was bought and then released by a Greek court physician. By another account, Persian king Darius having heard about the famous Greek granted him freedom. Anyway, after his release Pythagoras, now 56 years old, returned to Samos.

---

[46] **Iamblichus** (245-325) was a Syrian philosopher of Neoplatonism. In his 10-volume work dedicated to Pythagoreans he gave the most complete description of Pythagoras' life based on legends and a few historical documents.

[47] **Pherecydes** (flourished around 540 BC) was an ancient religion philosopher, who is credited with originating transmigration, a doctrine that holds the human soul to be immortal, passing into another body, either human, or animal, or even vegetable after death. Probably, he was the first person who ever wrote among the Greeks on the subject of Natural Philosophy and the Gods.

[48] **Thales of Miletus**, or **Thales the Milesian** (635-543 BC) was a pre-Socratic Greek philosopher and one of the Seven Sages of Greece. Many regard him as the first philosopher in the Greek tradition as well as the father of science.

[49] **Anaximander of Miletus** (610-546 BC) was the second of the physical philosophers of Ionia, a companion or pupil of Thales.

Pythagoras, who did not remain in Samos long because it was then under the rule of the tyrant[50] Polycrates, went to Croton (a town of the Greek colony in the Southern part of Apennine Peninsula), where, with a community of friends, he founded a half religious and half scientific brotherhood and school. That school was called the "*semicircle.*" Both men and women were permitted to become members of the semicircle. The school had many followers, but the "inner" circle of the school had a smaller number of philosophers and mathematicians who were called "*mathematikoi.*" These lived at the school in austere surroundings, had no possessions, and were [required to be] vegetarians. The Pythagoreans were famous for their mutual friendship, unselfishness, and honesty.

Pupils/disciples were admitted to Pythagoras' school only after completing successfully long and difficult tests. Candidates were required to form close friendships with the other students in keeping with Pythagoras' thinking that "a friend is an *alter ego* (*the second I*)," and that "friendship is harmonious equality." Before retiring for the night, the pupils were required to go over everything they had done or failed to do during the day: "Where did I misbehave, what did I do badly, what duty did I fail to accomplish?" They were taught by Pythagoras himself and obeyed strict rules. The beliefs that Pythagoras held were:

- Nature and the whole reality has an underlying mathematical structure
- Philosophy should be used for spiritual purification
- The soul, which is pure, can rise to experience the union with the divine
- Certain symbols (including mathematical) have a mystical significance.
- All brothers of the order should observe strict loyalty and secrecy.

Mathematikoi lived together, while the outer circle of followers, known as "*akousmatics*" lived with their own families and in their own homes, and attended the society's meetings and lectures during the day. They were not required to follow the strict rules as were the mathematikoi.

---

[50] Tyrant in ancient history - the name of a ruler who gained power by usurping the legal authority.

Pythagoreans were not structured like a research institution; rather they were a philosophical and religious brotherhood held together by the principle that mathematical truth lies at the root of all reality. That belief was their main motivation for studying mathematics and the properties of mathematical objects. They studied a varied array of subjects; mathematical classes were followed by musical exercises; musical exercises gave way to philosophical discussions…

Pythagoras was an accomplished astronomer of his time. For example, he believed the Earth to be a sphere, and, considering the body of knowledge of the time, we do not fault him for believing that it was located at the center of the Universe. Of those phenomena he could observe or measure, he often was remarkably correct. He realized that the orbit of the Moon is inclined to the equator of the Earth, and he was one of the first to realize that Venus as an evening star was the same planet as Venus, the morning star.

Pythagoras, a good musician who played the lyre, made remarkable contributions to the mathematical theory of music. He used music as a means to help those who were ill.

Iamblicus, already mentioned above, described the process by which Pythagoras arrived at the mathematical laws of musical harmony as follows: One day Pythagoras walked deep in thought trying to figure out how to construct a device to measure sounds in away that could be used to tune musical instruments. By chance, he happened to walk by the smithy and heard some simultaneous hammers hits, some of which made pleasant sounds while others did not. He ran into the smithy and inspected the hammers. He found that those hammers, whose weights formed simple proportions like 1:2 or 2:3 and so on, produced a pleasant harmonic sound.

Pythagoras studied properties of numbers, which would be familiar to mathematicians today, such as even and odd numbers, triangular numbers, perfect numbers, etc. Pythagoras believed that numbers had personalities, which certainly seems unacceptable in mathematics today: "Each number had its own personality – masculine or feminine, perfect or incomplete, beautiful or ugly. Ten is the very best number: it contains in itself the first four integers - one, two, three, and four, and these written in dot notation form a perfect triangle".

Pythagoreans introduced some special numbers that correspond to polygons. For instance, they have the so-called "triangular numbers", the construction of which becomes clear from the picture below.

Triangular numbers

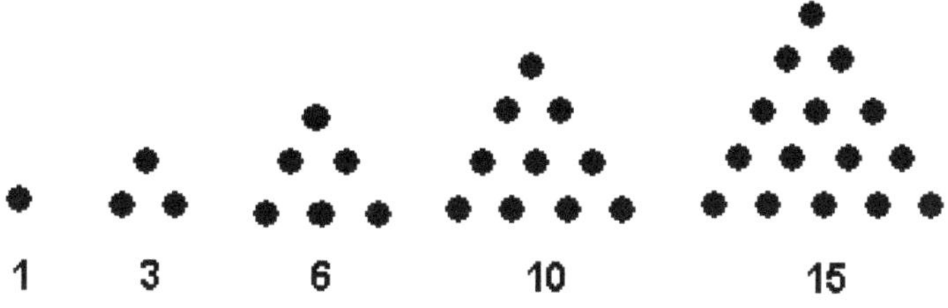

In the same manner, one can construct a set of "square numbers".

Square numbers

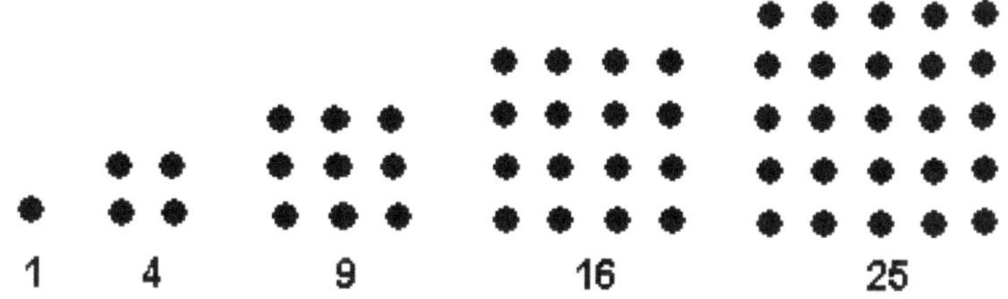

Pythagoreans also noticed that the sum of two neighboring triangular numbers is equal to a corresponding square number: for instance, 1+3=4, 3+6=9, and so on.

They already knew about a number of regular polygons:

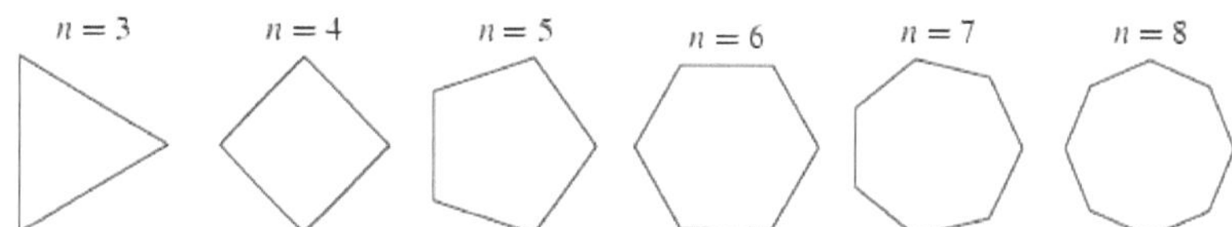

Thus, they introduced other polygonal numbers as well. Examples of the principle of construction of such numbers are given below.

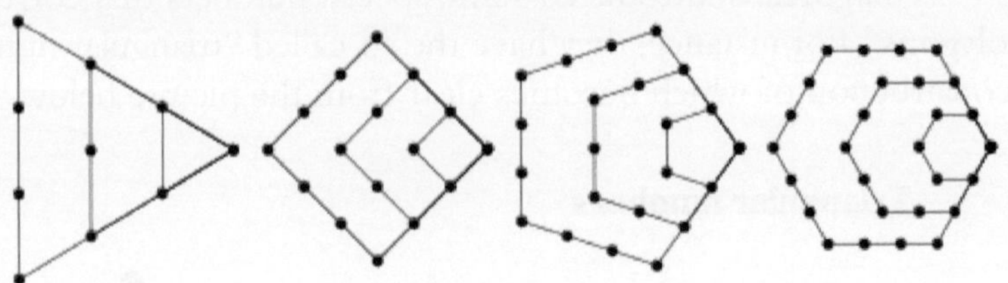

In addition to being known for their belief that numbers constitute the true nature of things, the Pythagoreans also are known for their theory of the transmigration of souls.

The Pythagoreans had unusual attitudes for that time. They believed that the sexes are equal, all slaves are to be treated humanely, and that animals should be respected as creatures with souls.

The highest purification of the soul was "philosophy," and Pythagoras has been credited with the first use of the term. It is interesting to notice that the Hippocratic Oath[51] – with its central commitment to "First do no harm" – has its roots in the oath of the Pythagorean Brotherhood.

Of course, today we particularly remember Pythagoras for his famous theorem in geometry. Although, we note that the theorem, now known as Pythagoras' theorem, was known to the Babylonians and Egyptians about 1000 years earlier. The right triangle with sides of 3 and 4 and the diagonal equal to 5, was known as the "Egyptian triangle." Ancient Egyptians took a rope with 11 evenly spaced knots and used it to make a right angle, for instance, on a land lot.

---

[51] **Hippocrates of Cos** (460 –380 BC) was the celebrated ancient Greek physician, commonly regarded as "the father of medicine." By legend, he belonged to the family that claimed descent from the mythical Aesculapius (Greek god of healing), son of one of the main Greek gods, Apollo. He is claimed the author of "*The Hippocratic Oath*", which traditionally taken by physicians up to modern days.

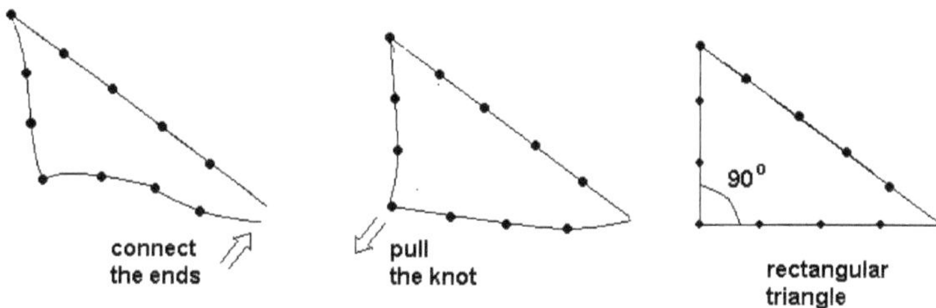

The first known proof of Pythagoras' Theorem belongs to Pythagoras. Whether Pythagoras himself proved this theorem is not known, as it was common in the ancient world to credit a famous teacher with the discoveries of his students. The earliest known mention of Pythagoras' name in connection with the theorem came five centuries after his death, in the writings of Cicero[52] and Plutarch[53].

Pythagoras' ideas had a tremendous impact, particularly on the young, and it was not long before he was accused of atheism and corruption of youth, charges of which he was eventually cleared.

Below are some extracts from "*The Golden Verses of Pythagoras*"

- First worship the immortal gods, in the manner prescribed.
- Respect the oath.
- Next, honor the reverent heroes[54] and the spirits of the dead
- Honor your parents and your relatives. As for others, befriend whoever excels in virtue.
- Yield to kind words and fruitful deeds, and do not hate your friend for a small fault where you are able.
- Do nothing shameful neither in the presence of others, nor privately
- Respect yourself above all.
- Practice justice in word and deed.
- If a lie is told, bear with it gently.
- Let no one persuade you by word or deed to do or say whatever is not best for you.
- Consider before acting, to avoid foolishness: it is the worthless man who speaks and acts thoughtlessly.

---

[52] **Marcus Tullius Cicero** (106-43 BC) was the greatest Roman orator, famous also as a politician and a philosopher. He was decapitated by his political rivals.
[53] **Plutarch** (46-127) was a famous Greek historian, biographer, and essayist.
[54] Heroes in the ancient Greece were half-gods (sometimes even mortal) as, for instance, Prometheus, Perseus, Hercules and others.

- Only perform such acts, as you will not regret later.
- Do not try to do anything of which you are ignorant, but learn what is necessary; in this way your life will be most pleasant.
- Practice a way of life that is pure, not dissipated, and guard against doing whatever incurs envy.
- Always do whatever will not harm you, and think before you act.
- Accustom thyself to a way of living that is neat and decent without luxury.
- Do not judge your height by the length of your shadow at sunset.
- Do not try to find your happiness: it is always inside yourself.
- Do great deeds; do not promise to do great deeds.
- Live in such a way that your friends never become your enemies though try make friends of your enemies.
- Life is like a theater: often not best people take the best places.
- A great ability to live happily is to live in the present.
- A man captured by his passions cannot be free.
- The beginning is half of the whole.
- It is equally dangerous to give a sword to a crazy man as it is to give power to a dishonest man.
- In arguments the words "yes" and "no" are extremely short; they need serious thought before being pronounced.
- Keep your children from crying, thus they will have tears left to drop on your grave.
- To live long, buy good old wine and save your old friend.

It is believed that Cylon, a powerful citizen of Croton, wanted to become a mathematikoi but Pythagoras refused him. This led to a whole-scale attack on Pythagoras and his followers, and, after the death of Pythagoras, to their ultimate persecution and demise.

As with most of the biographical information on Pythagoras, even the manner of his death is not certain: One story holds that he died in exile at Metapontum, a Greek colony on the shore of the Ionian Sea, and another holds that he was killed in an attack on his school by the citizens of Croton.

After Pythagoras' death, his wife Theano headed the Pythagorean Brotherhood, her three daughter and two sons helped her run the school. Theano was the first known woman-mathematician in history.

Leonardo Fibonacci (Leonardo Pisano)
(1175-1250)

Leonardo Fibonacci was one of the greatest mathematicians of medieval times.

He was probably the greatest genius in number theory in the 2000 years between Diophantus and Fermat.

Leonardo's full name is Leonardo of Pisa, or Leonardo Pisano in Italian, the name, as was typical of earlier times, indicating that he was born in Pisa (Italy). Leonardo of Pisa also is now known by his nick-name Fibonacci, which is a shortening of the Latin "*filius Bonacci,*" which means "the son of Bonacci." In turn, his father's name, "*Bonacci,*" means "a man of good nature."

Not surprisingly, little is known about Fibonacci's life. Even the only known portrait of Fibonacci was painted well after his death, so it is assumed that the painting reflects an image created on the basis of a verbal description... A hundred years or so later a statue of Leonardo was erected in his birthplace.

Nobody knows his exact date of birth; the general assumption is that he was born in 1175 in Pisa, Italy. His father, Guilielmo Bonacci, was a republic of Pisa diplomat who directed trade between Pisa and Bugia, Algeria (now it is Algerian port Bejaia). Around 1192 he brought Fibonacci to Bugia for schooling. He wanted Fibonacci to become a merchant so he sent his son to a school to major in mathematics. Fibonacci himself wrote, "When my father served as public notary in the customs office at Bugia I was still a child, and he summoned me to Bugia, because, with an eye on a useful future skill for me, he wanted me to stay there with him to attend accounting school. It was there that I was introduced to the art of the Indians' nine symbols through. This knowledge pleased me above all else and I came to understand it."

Fibonacci traveled extensively until about the year 1200, at which time he returned to Pisa and began to serve his birth-place city with is talents.

His most well known chef d'oeuvre, "*Liber abaci,*" (meaning "*Book of the Abacus*" or "*Book of Calculating*") was finished and published in 1202 and was then re-published in 1228. The book contains 15 chapters: About new Indian signs and their use for notation as numbers (Chapter 1); about addition, subtraction, multiplication and division of numbers (Chapters from 2 to 5); about arithmetical operations with fractions (Chapters from 6 to 7); about pricing of goods and the principles of exchange (Chapters from 8 to13); about finding square and cube roots (Chapter 14); and, at last, some knowledge on geometry and algebra (Chapter 15). By the way, this book contains the famous Fibonacci problem about rabbits that was considered in an earlier section in this book.

Fibonacci introduced the Hindu-Arabic positional decimal system and the use of Arabic numerals into Europe. His book persuaded many European mathematicians of his day to use the new system.

Fibonacci wrote several books which played an important role in reviving ancient mathematical skills as well as presenting significant contributions of his own. Fibonacci lived in the days before printing, so his books were hand-written and the only way to get a copy of one of his books was to have another hand-written copy made. Of his books we still have copies of "*Book of Calculating*" ("*Liber abaci*"), "*Practical Geometry*" ("*Practica geometriae*"), "*Flowers*" ("*Flos*") and "*Book on Square Numbers*" ("*Liber quadratorum*").

In 1220 Frederick II, an enlightened monarch who had been crowned Holy Roman emperor, became aware, through the scholars at his court, of Fibonacci's work. One member of Frederick's court, presented a number of problems as challenges to the great mathematician Fibonacci. Three of these problems were solved by Fibonacci, who wrote the answers in his book "*Flos,*" which he sent to Frederick II.

By the way, in "*Flos*" he solved the equation $10x + 2x^2 + x^3 = 20$ with a remarkable degree of accuracy. Without explaining his methods, Fibonacci gave the approximate solution in Babylonian notation as 1.22.7.42.33.4.40 (this is written to base 60, so it is $1+\frac{22}{60}+\frac{7}{60^2}+\frac{42}{60^3}+...$). This converts to the decimal 1.3688081075 which is correct to nine decimal places. A remarkable achievement!

"*Liber quadratorum*", written in 1225, is Fibonacci's most impressive piece of work, although not the work for which he is most famous. The book was dedicated to number theory, in which, among other things, he examined methods for finding Pythagorean triples. Fibonacci first notes that square numbers can be constructed as sums of odd numbers, essentially describing an inductive construction using the formula $n^2 + (2n+1) = (n+1)^2$. In "*Liber quadratorum*" Fibonacci wrote, "I thought about the origin of all square numbers and discovered that they arose from the regular ascent of odd numbers. For unity is a square and from it is produced the first square, namely 1; adding 3 to this makes the second square, namely 4, which root is 2; if to this sum is added a third odd number, namely 5, the third square will be produced, namely 9, which root is 3; and so a sequence of square numbers is generated through the regular addition of odd numbers."

Constructing Pythagorean triples, Fibonacci proceeded as follows: "Thus when I wish to find two square numbers which addition produces a square number, I take any odd square number as one of the two square numbers and I find the other square number by the addition of all the odd numbers from unity up to but excluding the odd square number. For example, I take 9 as one of the two squares mentioned; the remaining square will be obtained by the addition of all the odd numbers below 9, namely 1, 3, 5, 7, which sum is 16, a square number, which when added to 9 gives 25, a square number". Fibonacci also proves many interesting number theory results such as: (1) there is no x, y such that $x^2 + y^2$ and $x^2 - y^2$ are both squares; (2) $x^4 - y^4$ cannot be a square, and others.

Fibonacci's work in number theory was almost wholly ignored and virtually unknown during the Middle Ages.

There is the only existing document which refers to Fibonacci. That document is a decree issued by the Republic of Pisa in 1240 that awards a salary to "... the serious and learned Master Leonardo Bigollo ..." (Bigollo means "traveler"; it was yet another nickname for Fibonacci.) This salary was given to Fibonacci in recognition for the services that he had given to the city as advisor on matters of accounting and instruction of the citizens.

Nothing is known about his death. A coined version that he was killed during the 5th Crusade while accompanying Frederick the 2nd in 1228 is evidently in conflict with the above quoted document.

Fra Luca Bartolomeo de Pacioli (1445 - 1517)

Luca Pacioli with his pupil

Italian monk and mathematician, a friend and teacher of Leonardo a Vinci. The author of famous tractates "*Divina proportione* and *Summa de arithmetica.*

The second of this tractate contains main principles of accounting for what Pacioli is often referred as "The Father of Accounting".

In 1869 the Milan Accounting Academy asked one of their members to present a lecture on the history of accounting. That man while preparing the lecture accidentally found a Medieval tractate written by a then unknown author, Luca Pacioli. One of the chapters of the tractate included the first published description of the method of keeping accounts used by Venetian merchants and known as the double-entry accounting system. It was the first modern glimpse into Pacioli. Since then historians have gathered data about "The Father of Accounting" and reconstructed his biography.

* * * * *

Luca Pacioli was born in 1445 in a small Italian town of Borgo Santo Sepulcro, which name means "The city of the Holy Coffin." In his early years, Pacioli helped one of the local merchants by doing his accounting. However, his father, who was a respected man in the city, found that his son had some ability in painting and arranged for his son to study in the studio of the famous Italian painter Piero della Francesca.[55],

who was at the same time a bit of a mathematician. It was his teacher's math ability that proved more influential on Pacioli than his teacher's painting ability. As one of Pacioli's biographers wrote: "The number for Pacioli as well as for his teacher seemed to be a universal key that opened access simultaneously to truth and beauty".

When he was around 20 years old, at the suggestion and facilitation of Alberti[56], a friend of della Francesca, Pacioli left his home city to take on the position of tutor to a rich Venetian merchant. Simultaneously he attended lectures on mathematics.

In six years Alberti invited Pacioli to be his guest in Rome. Pacioli still was undecided about his focus and in about two years he left Alberti's house.

In 1472 at age of 27, Pacioli still had not become successful in his career/life, so he decided to become a Franciscan monk. He accepted a sacrament of mendacity and was given a new name – fra Luca di Borgo San Sepolcro.

After that he lived in his own home town. His teacher della Francesca in 1475 painted the picture "Madonna with a Child," in which it is assume that Pacioli, was used as a model for Saint Peter (he is shown in the middle of the picture below).

At that time Pacioli began to write his encyclopedic tractate, "*Summa de Arithmetica, Geometria, proportioni et Proportionalita*".

Due to his scientific activity, in 1477 he became a professor at Perugia University. Evidently, he was a good teacher because in a year the University's "council" of professors noted that "due to the necessity to have such a scientist and experienced lecturer of mathematics and taking

---

[55] **Piero della Francesca** (1415 – 1492) was an Italian painter and art theoretician of the Early Renaissance.

[56] **Leon Batista Alberti** (1404 - 1472)was an Italian scientist, writer and outstanding architect of Renaissance.

into account his virtue and morality," they offered him a two year position with double salary.

In 1493, after 13 years of hard work, he finished his "*Summa de Arithmetica*" and published this work with support from the local Venetian ruler. Only seven copies of this book are left today. This book, with over 300 pages, was divided into 5 parts: Arithmetic and Algebra; Commerce; Accounting; Weights, measures and interest; Geometry.

A part of the book "Tractate on Accounting and Recording" is considered now as the first theoretical book on accounting.

The book immediately brought Pacioli publicity and notoriety. So, when in 1496 the largest Italian city, Milan, established the University, Pacioli was invited to head the department of mathematics. Simultaneously he taught mathematics at the court of the duke of Milan, Ludovico Sforza. At the same time the most brilliant scientist of the time, Leonardo da Vinci, was among those at the duke's court.

Naturally, Pacioli and Leonardo, having much in common, quickly became close friends. Mathematics and art were areas of their discussions at length, and both of them gained greatly from each other. At this time Pacioli began work on the second of his famous works, "*Divina proportione*" and the figures for the text were drawn by Leonardo. Actually, Leonardo intended to write an analogous book but being impressed by Pacioli's work, decided to be an illustrator to his book.

In 1499 the French army occupied Milan, and both scientists left Milan for Florence, where their paths separated. Within two years Pacioli became the head of the mathematical department at the University in Bologna, the oldest European university.

In four years Pacioli again returned to Florence, with the brotherhood of the Saint Cross monastery. He dedicated all his free time to the translation of Euclid's[57] "Elements" and to the completion of his own "Divina Propocione".

The translation of Euclid was published in 1508. The book was met without enthusiasm. At the same time his own book in which he

---

[57] **Euclid** (315 – 255 BC.) was a famous ancient mathematician, the author of the first mathematical works. In his main work "Elements" considered axiomatic construction of geometry.

used all illustrations by Leonardo and personal conversations with his teacher Piero della Francesca became quite successful.

Little is known about the last years of Pacioli's life except that he lived at the Saint Cross monastery and subsequently, Papal approval, became a priest in his home town.

For many years the date of his death was not known. It was only recently that Japanese historians found in church records that he died in Florence in 1517. Pacioli was buried in his town of San Sepulcro in the church, which building still stands today… but which is used as storage…

*****

At the end of 19th century, when Pacioli was known world-wide, on the wall of San Sepulcro's administrative building a memorial plaque was erected: "To Luca Pacioli, who was a friend and advisor to Leonardo da Vinci, who gave algebra a tongue and developed geometry, who discovered the double-entry accounting system and opened the way for future discoveries. Citizens of the town of San Sepulcro, to correct 370 years of neglect build this memorial to their great compatriot."

Leonardo da Vinci

(1452 - 1519)

Non mi legga, chi non matematico nelli mia principi. (Do not read my works if you are not a mathematician.)

Leonardo

Italian polymath: painter, sculptor, architect, musician, scientist, mathematician, engineer, inventor, anatomist, geologist, cartographer, botanist and writer.

Leonardo has often been described as the archetype of the Renaissance man. He is widely considered to be one of the greatest painters of all time and perhaps the most diversely talented person ever to have lived.

Many mysterious and enigmatic stories are connected with the Great Man of the Renaissance – Leonardo da Vinci. The first of them began with his birth: He was an illegitimate child of a woman about whom we know nothing except that her name was Catarina and that she was a peasant. His father, Pierro da Vinci, was a hereditary notary.

The Vincis lived in the small town of Vinci (west of Florence), where Leonardo was born. During the Renaissance, society was tolerant of illegitimate children, and Leonardo's father recognized his son and even attended his baptism, after which Leonardo and his mother were sent to the nearby village of Anchiano, where they stayed about four years. In keeping with customs of the time, Leonardo's mother was given with a dowry and was given in marriage to a local peasant. Meanwhile, Leonardo's father married a young 16-year old girl of noble descent. But this couple was childless, so Leonardo was taken back into his father's home. Leonardo, a handsome and clearly smart boy with a friendly disposition became a favorite of the family. He was afforded a good education, and he demonstrated excellent abilities in drawing.

When Leonardo was 15 years old, his father moved to Florence and took his son with him. Because he was an illegitimate son, he could not become a judge or a doctor, so his father decided to make him an artist. (At that time artists were considered to be craftsmen and occupied a place in society alongside tailors.) Leonardo began an apprenticeship in the workshop of Andrea del Verrocchio[58] who was at this time the most gifted and manifold artist in Florence. Verrocchio was fascinated by young Leonardo's drawings, so he took Leonardo into his workshop. Some of Leonardo's contemporaries at the workshop included the famous artists Boticelli[59] and Perugino[60].

At 20 years old, Leonardo already was recognized by his tutor and the public as a singular talent in painting. In 1472 Leonardo was listed in the red book of painters from Florence. Leonardo's apprenticeship ended when he became a full member of the Florentine painters' guild of St. Luke. Even after his "graduation," Leonardo continued to live with Verrocchio's family.

A scandalous event happened in 1476. In those days it was usual to put anonymous accusations in a wooden box, which was put up in front of the City Hall. Leonardo and four others artists from Verrocchio's studio were accused of having a homosexual affair («*Peccato di Sodomia*») with a boy, who was a model. Within six months from the initial accusation the anonymous accusation was repeated. At that time the punishment for Sodomy was very severe; an accused potentially could be burned to death in the city square. The trial was held, but no evidence was presented, so all defendants were acquitted of the charge. Despite the acquittal, all of the defendants were whipped (presumable, to demonstrate official power). It was suspected that somebody decided to settle a score with one of Verrocchio's pupils.

---

[58] **Andrea del Verrocchio** (1436–1488) was an Italian sculptor and painter of Early Renaissance living in Florence. (His real name was **Andrea di Michele di Francesco de' Cioni.**) He was a pupil of jewelry master Verrocchio whose name became a basis of his nickname.

[59] **Sandro Botticelli** (1445–1510) was one of the most prominent painters of Renaissance.

[60] **Pietro Perugino (Vannucci)** (1445-1523) was an Italian painter of Early Renaissance.

In 1482 Leonardo moved to Milan. In his letter to the ruler of Milan, Lodovico Sforza, he represented himself as an engineer and military expert as well as a painter.

For a salary less than that of a court jester's he performed the duties of a military engineer, hydraulic technician, court painter and architect. These years in Milan were filled with various deeds. Leonardo painted a famous fresco on the wall of the refectory at the Dominican monastery Santa-Maria delle Gracie in Milan – "*The Last Supper*" where Jesus is depicted at the very culminating moment telling, "Verily I say into you, that one of you shall betray me".

In 1500 there was a terrible flood and the monastery that stood in the low place was partially under water. The unique fresco began to be destroyed almost immediately after its creation; the colors began to wash away… Already, by the middle of the 16th century only spots remained of the original painting. In 16th and 17th centuries the fresco was restored several times, however, unsuccessfully. The last restoration was done in the middle of the 20th century, and the fresco at last has some likeness to its original.

While painting, Leonardo also spent much time on inventions, and he began faithfully to write down all his engineering ideas. From his notes, one can see that Leonardo worked in many different areas: architecture, anatomy, hydraulics, mechanics and even theatrical decorations. Although many of his projects were brilliant and were centuries ahead of his time, to be balanced, we note that he rarely completed his projects.

Leonardo also studied Euclid and Pacioli's "Suma" and began his own study of geometry, sometimes creating mechanical solutions to problems. Around this time, he wrote a book on the elementary theory of mechanics, which appeared in Milan around 1498.

When the French drove Lodovico Sforza from Milan in 1499, Leonardo moved to Venice and then back to Florence. It is known that he was so strongly absorbed by mathematics that he even hated to take a brush in hand. For twelve years Leonardo moved from town to town, performing different engineering projects.

In Florence he involved himself in a competition with the young genius Michelangelo[61], who was only 25 years old at the moment. The culmination of this rivalry seemed to be the battle scene paintings, one by Leonardo and one by Michelangelo, for the *palazzo della Signoria (*also called *palazzo Vecchio* that means "*Old Palace*"). Unfortunately, these paintings by the two geniuses disappeared during "restoration" of the palace by the known architect Vasary[62], who preferred to put his own frescos on the walls of the palace. During this time, Leonardo created one of his best known chef d'oeuvres – the portrait of Mona Lisa (an abbreviation of Madonna Lisa) also known as La Gioconda. Mona Lisa was the third wife of Florentine merchant Francesco di Bartolomee del Giocondo. The Mona Liza also known as "La Joconde" in French is in the Louvre, in Paris. When Mona Lisa modeled for the portrait she was about 24 years old an already mature age for that time. Leonardo did not try to paint a beauty (obviously, Mona Lisa was not really a beauty); instead, he concentrated on capturing the lady's character.

The Mona Lisa remained an object of study primarily by professional art experts until 1911 when it was stolen from the Louvre. The painting remained hidden by the robbers for three years before it was recovered and returned to the Louvre. All this time the European media published pictures of Leonardo's masterpiece, contributing to its recognition and fame.

Leonardo wrote down his ideas from painting to anatomy, from mathematics to the theory flight. One interesting aspect of his handwriting is that he wrote from right to left, so his manuscripts could be read more easily with the use of a mirror than otherwise; he wrote his letters in the usual manner, though, so a mirror image was not a normal image. Leonardo's biographers assume that he did this to keep his works private from wandering eyes.

In 1513 Leonardo's protectors were driven out of Milan, and Leonardo went to Rome where he spent three years under the protection of Lorenzo Medici[63]. French kings admired Italian Renaissance artifacts,

---

[61] **Michelangelo Buonarroti** in full **Michelangelo di Lodovico Buonarroti Simoni** (1475-1564) was an Italian sculptor, painter, architect, poet and philosopher. One of the great masters of the Renaissance. He made frescos on the ceiling of the Sistine Chapel in Vatican City.

[62] **Giorgio Vasari** (1511–1574) was an Italian painter, architect and writer.

[63] **Lorenzo di Piero de Medici** (1449-1492), nicknamed Lorenzo the Magnificent, was an Italian statesman and ruler of the Florentine Republic during the Italian Renaissance.

especially Leonardo's "*The Last Supper*," so it was no surprise that in 1516 Francis I[64], already being acquainted with Leonardo's art, invited the artist to his court. Though officially Leonardo was responsible of an hydraulic project at the king's palace, his main duties were as court advisor.

Leonardo died in 1519 in Aboise, the residency of the French kings in those days. He was buried in the heart of the king's castle, in the cloister of San Fiorentino. In the turmoil of the French religious wars and revolutions, the cemetery where Leonardo was buried fell into state of neglect. Furthermore, gravestones were used for building construction, coffin covers were removed, and even the bones of the deceased ended up being jumbled together. In the beginning of the 19th century one of Leonardo's admirers tried to extract Leonardo's remains from the common grave for a proper reburial. He decided that he could identify Leonardo's bones by choosing those bones that would correspond to a man of the right height and skull size because Leonardo was a handsome and intelligent man. Those "selected' remains were buried in the Chapel of St. Hubert, which is situated inside the area of the king's castle in Amboise. Now guides point to the grave and tell visitors that it is Leonardo's grave… though that may not be correct.

Thus, three centuries after Leonardo's death, there is yet one more mystery connected to Leonardo; there could be remains of two people or maybe even 10… Does at least one bone belong to Leonardo?

* * *

The term "Renaissance man" is associated with Leonardo da Vinci; none of his contemporaries – even most brilliant and talented – can be compared with him. He was a great painter though had made only twelve paintings. He was a musician who was capable on nearly all known instruments of his day. He was a composer-improvisator. He was a poet and a writer who could amuse the public with unexpected and impromptu presentations. For instance, he wrote the following clever mini-fable: "A paper, upon looking at itself, covered with writing became furious. The

---

Sponsor of art and science. The Medici family of Florence can be traced back to the end of the 12th century. They were a part of the patrician class. The root of their family name lays probably in the fact that one of them was a doctor (medico) at the Charles the Great (Karolus Magnus) court.

[64] **Francis I** (1494-1547) was the King of France.

inkpot silenced the paper, quipping that 'without the writing nobody would keep you at all.' "

A simple enumeration of Leonardo's professional interests beyond art is amazing: anatomy, botany, cartography, geology, mathematics, aeronautics, optics, astronomy, hydraulics, acoustics, civil architecture, weapons design, and city planning...

The heritage left to us by Leonardo is very interesting. With no intent to cover all his works, we would like to mention some of his projects that – alas – were never completed in his time. His notes of these inventions remained in private collections for several centuries hidden from the world.

* * *

Leonardo was preoccupied all his life with he thought of human flight. He wrote, "Though a human is a skilled inventor… he never makes an object more beautiful, simpler, nor more perfect than Nature." In a sense, that conviction directed Leonardo to invent an avionic machine that imitates the operation of a bird wing– the so-called "ornicopter." Unfortunately, human muscles are not strong enough to make this idea viable.

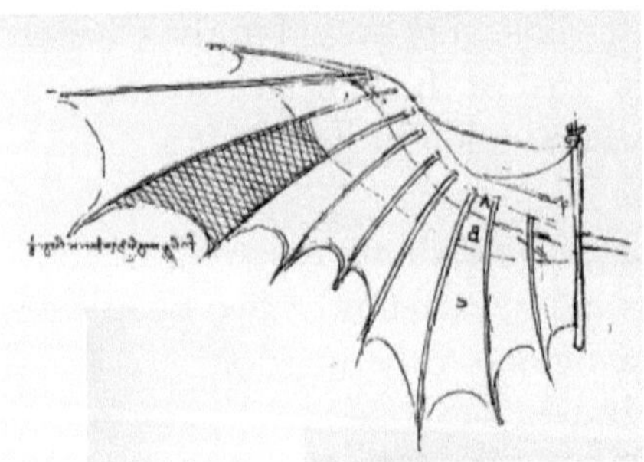

Model ofthe wing (Leonardo's drawing).

Nevertheless, Leonardo invented the very first avionic device that is a predecessor of the modern delta planes. It was to be controlled by the human body.

He wrote on this occasion: "A man with an avionic device has to keep his upper body free for movement so that he can balance as if in a boat."

He was first to design an aerodynamic propeller that is considered to be the first model of a helicopter.

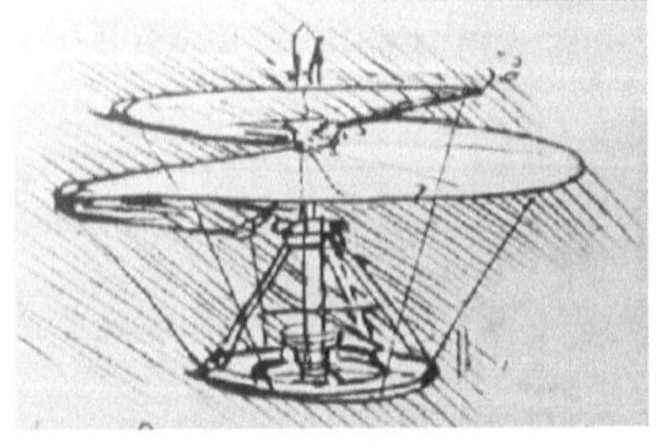

The first parachute is also his invention.

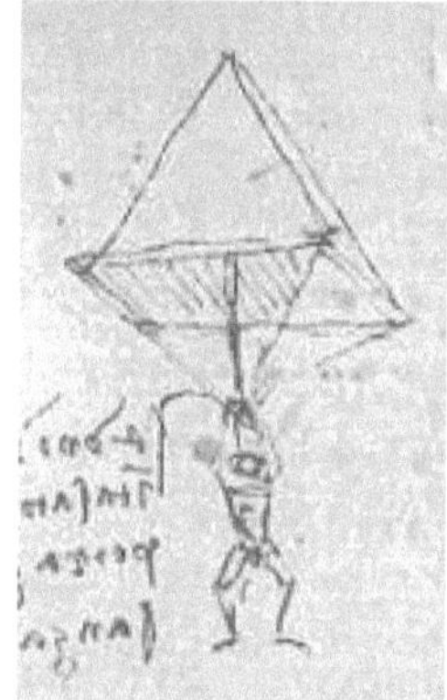

Water was the second area that interested the great inventor. He invented gloves in the form of duck feet for swimming.

There already existed systems for working under water. For instance, Alexander the Great descended to the sea bottom under a huge bell. However, Leonardo went further; he invented a diving-suit. The system of tubes that connected it with the water surface allowed staying under the water as long as needed. Those tubes were supported by corks or leather bags with air. Of course, the depth of such dives was severely limited because water pressure on the human diaphragm makes all but very shallow depth excursions impossible.

Leonardo invented the ubiquitous lifesaver or ring buoy.

He invented a number of devices for military use. For example, Leonardo invented a tank, which he described as follows: "I will make covered chariots that will be safe and invulnerable. This chariot has to be followed by infantry-men who will be defended by this vehicle." He designed a chariot in the form of a tortilla armored with metallic shields and an armed turret on the top of it. Inside the chariot is an "engine" consisting of 8 soldiers who turn the wheels. He designed cannon with a mechanism for controlling angles (vertical and horizontal). He also invented a 33-barrel cannon that could fire many shots without reloading. To improve firing accuracy, he invented shells with stabilizers.

Although catapults were known since ancient times, it was Leonardo who critically improved them by making a regulator to control the force of action. He also invented mobile staircases used for storming an enemy's defending walls.

Of course, we touched on only a small part of Leonardo's inventions; he left about 20,000 pages of manuscripts, from which about 7000 have survived to date. Each page contains descriptions and schemes …

Leonardo was also interested in astronomy. He certainly realized the possibility of constructing a telescope. In "*Codex Atlanticus*" written in 1490 he talks of "making glasses to see the Moon enlarged." In a later work "*Codex Arundul*" written in about 1513, he says that "in order to observe the nature of the planets, open the roof and bring the image of a single planet onto the base of a concave mirror. The image of the planet reflected by the base will show the surface of the planet much magnified."

And many other inventions and brilliant ideas are beyond this brief exposition …

* * *

Leonardo's aphorisms

- You can love only that you have known.
- If one has no valid arguments to present, he resorts to shouting.
- Where there is no hope, there is emptiness.
- Nature is arranged in such a way that everybody has to learn something new.
- An enemy who shows you your mistakes is more useful than a friend who tries to hide them from you.
- Who lives with fear will perish from fear.
- There are always eyes and ears for your secrets.
- Even a lion has bad days.
- A well lived day gives a good sleep; a usefully lived life gives a peaceful death.
- Who does not punish evil helps to create more of it.
- Persistence will triumph over all obstacles.
- Science is the general and practice is the soldier.
- By insulting others you insult yourself.
- We have got from our parents the priceless gift – our life. They devoted their love and strength to help us grow. And now, when they are old and ill, our obligation is to take care of them!
- He who does not care about life does not deserve life.
- The food for your old age is your wisdom, so behave in your youth in such a way, so your old age will not be hungry.
- You can cause harm when you bless something, however you an cause even more harm even more harm when blame something that you don't understand.
- Iron rusts without use; water begins to foul when it stagnates; as well, a human mind without use deteriorates.
- Where an artist's hand is not directed by the soul, there is no art.
- The root of studying is bitter though the fruit is sweet.
- A real love is seen during unhappiness. It is like a light: the darker a night, the brighter the light.
- Knowledge gained without practice is fruitless and erroneous.
- It is better to die than to suffer in slavery.
- Only a usefully lived life is really long.
- Happiness is the destiny of those who work hard.
- Glory is in hands of labor.
- If you criticize something, criticize the opinion, not the author.
- Anger is a short-lived madness.

Self-advertising page

You can buy the following my books of series "Legends and Stories about mathematical Insights" in English:

These books can be found at http://www.lulu.com/shop/ in search window choose "BOOK", then in the next window type "USHAKOV". Make your choice!

At the same site you can find another my books.

www.ingramcontent.com/pod-product-compliance
Ingram Content Group UK Ltd.
Pitfield, Milton Keynes, MK11 3LW, UK
UKHW041935190726
13854UKWH00004B/1598

9 781105 883194